CW01433583

Newstead by Stamford
Priory

Newstead by Stamford Priory

N J Sheehan

Stamford

2018

© 2018 N J Sheehan
Published by N J Sheehan
Printed by Spiegl Press Ltd, Stamford
ISBN 978-0-9575038-5-4

For my family

Contents

Figures and Tables

Preface

Newstead by Stamford Priory in Uffington parish suffered the fate of the majority of monasteries at the Dissolution and went the way of so many smaller houses of Augustinian canons by disappearing almost without trace. There is negligible awareness of the priory and even its precise location is uncertain. Crucial clues provided by earthworks at the west end of Uffington Park offered a starting point to explore the physical nature, national importance and ultimate demise of this little-known religious house.

Nicholas J Sheehan
November 2018

Acknowledgements

I am grateful to the many people who assisted me with this study.

My particular thanks are due to Dr David Robinson for his scholarly advice and for commenting on a late version of the manuscript.

I am also indebted to the following for their valuable contributions:

Peter Foden, Archivist to the Duke of Rutland, Belvoir Castle

Prof Robert N Swanson, Emeritus Professor of Medieval Ecclesiastical History, University of Birmingham

Adam Daubney, Lincolnshire Finds Liaison Officer for the Portable Antiquities Scheme

Mark Bennet, Senior Historic Environment Record Officer, LINCSSMR

Richard Watts, Historic Environment Assistant (Records), Planning Services, Lincolnshire County Council

Graham Deacon, Archive Services Officer, Historic England

Prof Stephen Upex, Archaeologist and Landscape Historian, Institute of Continuing Education, University of Cambridge

Prof David Stocker, Hon Visiting Professor of Medieval Studies, University of Leeds

Lady Christine de la Rue, custodian of the archive of the Uffington Berties

John Hopson, Archivist, Stamford Town Hall

The staff of Lincolnshire Archives

The staff of Stamford Library, especially Jane Barber

Any errors of fact or interpretation committed in the compilation of this account are my responsibility alone.

1. Background

One mile to the west of Uffington village, at the parish boundary with Stamford, is the hamlet of Newstead (Fig.1). For around 300 years in the Middle Ages, this was the location of an Augustinian priory.

Fig.1 Map of Uffington and Newstead (Free online ordnance survey map and public footpath finder UK)

2. Newstead by Stamford Priory

Newstead Priory in the parish of Uffington was originally founded as a hospital by William de Albini III[1] (after 1146–1236), great grandson of Norman nobleman Robert de Todeni who came to England with William the Conqueror (Sheehan [a]). Established near the end of the twelfth century (Dugdale; Dickinson [a] (i)), or in the early-thirteenth century (Franklin M J), in honour of the Blessed Virgin Mary, 'at the bridge of Wass[2] between Stamford and Offington' (Dugdale), it has been known variously as De Novo Loco iuxta Stanford, Ad pontem de Uffington (Tanner), Newstead by Stamford (Page[a]) and Newstede by Uffington (Gill).

The title 'Novo Loco'[3], or 'Newstead', was shared by two other priories in the English East Midlands, namely Newstead Priory in Nottinghamshire, established in about 1170 (Page [b]), and the Gilbertine Newstead-on-Ancholme in Lincolnshire, founded in 1171 (Page [c]). Particular care must be taken to avoid confusing the Uffington and Nottinghamshire houses, both of which were Augustinian priories dedicated to the Blessed Virgin Mary. The former was referred to more specifically and unequivocally as Novo Loco iuxta Stanford (Salter HE).

Footnotes

1. Alternatively, d'Aubigné

2. Nowadays the Gwash

3. 'New Place' or 'new monastery' (Cameron)

3. Foundation by William de Albini III

Born at Belvoir Castle in about 1151 (Vincent), Willliam de Albini III (Fig.2) was a distinguished soldier who served under Richard the Lionheart in Normandy in 1194. In 1215, along with other discontented barons, he took up arms against King John (for which he was excommunicated by the pope), and he was one of the 25 sureties of Magna Carta at Runnymede (Sheehan [a]). Eventually compelled to surrender after holding the castle of Rochester against the monarch, de Albini was imprisoned in punishment for his part in the rebellion, and his manor in Uffington and castle at Belvoir were confiscated by the Crown. The Uffington manor was restored to him the following year on payment of a ransom by his second wife, Agatha Trussebut.

After reconciling with the Crown, de Albini commanded an army of Henry III at the second Battle of Lincoln in 1217, and he was one of the group of counsellors who witnessed the final and definitive reissue of Magna Carta and the Charter of the Forest in 1225 (Magna Carta Barons Association). He lived out the remaining years of his life in peace, dying at Uffington in 1236 (Peck (i)). It was probably during his retirement that he founded Newstead by Stamford. Although initially a home, or hospital, for 'seven poor, weak and infirm persons of sound faith and honest life', provision was made to add to the number of residents should the wealth of the

Fig.2 Arms of William de Albini III

hospital increase (Peck (ii)). The founder stipulated that it should be a house of regular canons living according to the Rule of St Augustine.

Willliam de Albini III endowed the house with the site of the bridge chapel of the Blessed Mary at Newstead, the adjacent house (or court), and his Uffington mill and its appurtenances (Dugdale). He also bestowed numerous parcels of land in Uffington and over a wider area, few of whose place names are recognisable now (Peck (ii)). The pasture that he donated was sufficient for 100 sheep, six oxen, six cows and two bulls (Dugdale). Additionally, he pledged a tithe of the bread, meat, fish and wax of his household. When the number of beds was later increased to 13, he gave another 45 acres or so of land in Uffington, a collective rent of 3s.3d, nine hens and three cocks yearly from his tenants Richard de Middleton, William Cok, William son of Thurstan, and William Snell, and further rents of 45s. from two other parishes (Dugdale). These gifts and grants were ratified by his son William de Albini IV (d.1242) and his granddaughter Isabel[1] de Ros (c.1233–1301) (Willis, F E d'A), and they were ultimately confirmed by Edward III in a parliament held at Stamford in 1337 (Dugdale). In her charter dated 25 December 1298, Isabel added the right to fish in the Gwash, together with a gallon of beer from all her tenants (Willis, F E d'A).[2]

No foundation charter is known to exist for Newstead by Stamford but there is little evidence for the house before the 1220s (Franklin M J). The name 'de Nouo Loco' first appeared in connection with Uffington's Newstead in 1210 in the unpublished

Feet of Fines (Cameron), but this might relate to when the monastery was first mooted or preliminary discussions were taking place. De Albini would scarcely have had time to establish a religious house when he was still an active soldier or while serving as sheriff in several counties (Sheehan [a]). It is more likely that it was instituted after he had fought at the Battle of Lincoln in 1217, and even after he had witnessed the final version of Magna Carta in 1225. The first charter of William III and his wife Agatha, dated to between 1226 and 1232 (Franklin M J), records the establishment of the hospital under its master, Adam, with the consent of Bishop Hugh of Lincoln and Archdeacon Robert of Lincoln (Dugdale). Because Hugh of Wells was bishop from 1209 to 1235 (Greenway), and Robert de Hayles was archdeacon from about 1223 to 1238 (Willis, Browne), this confirms that the hospital was inaugurated somewhere between 1223 and 1235. Eighteenth- and nineteenth-century writers concurred that the house was founded about the year 1230 (Peck (ii); Harrod; Drakard; Walcott).

As with the foundation date of the hospital, the point at which it became a fully conventual priory can only be approximated. Its conversion from hospital to priory was covertly indicated by a few significant changes in terminology in the house's charters, such as the substitution of 'canons' for 'brothers' and 'prior' for 'master' (Dickinson [a] (ii)). Because the transition occurred at the instigation of William de Albini IV (Dugdale), the hospital must have become a priory between his father's death in 1236 and his own death in 1242.

Footnotes

1. Alternatively, Isabella

2. The whereabouts of this charter are unknown. It was witnessed by Isabel's sons, William, the first* baron, Robert, appointed Treasurer to the King's Exchequer in 1285, Peter de Ros, Precentor of York, and Nicholas de Ros, Rector of Uffington (Willis, F E d'A).

*Willis described William as the second Baron de Ros but it is now accepted that he was the first on the grounds that the writ conferring the honour on his father was ultimately deemed to be invalid (Sheehan [b] (i)).

4. Location of the Priory

Surprisingly, the precise location of Newstead by Stamford remains uncertain. Like those of very many other smaller houses of Augustinian canons (Dickinson [b]), its buildings gradually disappeared after the Dissolution of the Monasteries, leaving little except unexplored foundations below ground. These days, the most prominent landmark at Newstead is the Grade II-listed former steam and water corn mill, which was built in the early-nineteenth century but is believed to have been erected in the position of the previous medieval water mill.

William de Albini III founded the hospital 'at the bridge of the Wass between Stanford and Offington' in 'the place in which the chapel of the blessed Mary is situate' (Peck (ii)). Similarly, William de Albini IV referred to 'the church of S. Mary of New-Place at the bridge of Uffintun' (Peck (iii)). This location is corroborated by antiquary John Leland who stated in *Itinerary*, written when the priory was still standing, that: 'This Newstede is withyn lesse then a mile beneth Stanford, but not hard apon the ryver' (Smith, LT). The priory is said to have been sited close to the water mill (Harrod; Burton, Geo). It might therefore be supposed that the priory buildings were clustered between the bridge chapel and the mill to its north-west. However, a field examination conducted by the Ordnance Survey in 1962 found no surface traces of Newstead Priory in the vicinity of Newstead Mill (Lincolnshire County Council), and in the 1990s the RCHME[1] National Mapping Programme, based on aerial photography, found no evidence whatsoever of Newstead Priory (Historic England).

It has long been believed locally that the priory was situated at the west end of what is now Uffington Park. When a quantity of relics was discovered in 1863 by labourers constructing a new carriage drive from the turnpike road to Uffington House in the centre of the village, the find was said to place the priory firmly on the east side of the River Gwash, near the bridge, thereby removing any remaining doubts about its location (*Mercury* [a]). Sadly, the precise position was not specified. An unpublished essay written in 1892 posited that 'the hospital appears to have stood on the opposite side of the road to the present mill, in a corner of the park of the Earl of Lindsey, where undulations and ridges in the ground probably define the site of the old foundations' (STH [a]). Based on the position of these earthworks, Uffington rector Rev F Earle d'A Willis concluded that the exact location was within the park on the right (as viewed from the road) of the Horse Shoe Hurn gate[2] (Willis, F E d'A); this is about a quarter of a mile from the present Newstead bridge, which replaced the medieval structure. It is a reasonable assumption that the route of the carriage drive is shown by the present farm track that runs from the Stamford–Deepings road to join the western end of the lime tree avenue of the lost Uffington House, where it terminates on reaching Stamford Canal.[3] In past times, the turnpike road connecting Stamford and Uffington ran around the north side of Newstead spinney (Fig.3) which was then part of Uffington Park. Meeting the Ryhall road (now Newstead Lane) at the bottom of the hill by the corner cottage, the road bridged the river behind the old turnpike house (Willis, F E d'A). This would place the earlier bridge[4] roughly 75 yards from the present crossing over the Gwash. The medieval stone bridge, which had four arches, was nearly 110 feet in length with a carriageway that narrowed to less than 14 feet in width (STH [b]). Although parts of it were 'in a dilapidated and ruinous state' in 1823 (STH [b]), the old bridge was not replaced until the early 1830s (STH [c]). Because the trustees of the turnpike road were responsible for the approaches to both ends of the river crossing, the road will have been diverted south of the spinney at the same time as the new bridge was erected. It is not known whether any structural remains or other artefacts associated with the priory were uncovered during the replacement of the bridge and re-routing of the road, but it is possible that remnants of its buildings and their contents (if not the greater part of the remains of the priory) lie under Newstead Spinney and the main road.[5]

Fig.3 Ordnance Survey 1824 map

An indication of the ground plan of the portion of the priory putatively located to the south of Newstead Bridge is provided by a Google Earth satellite image of the earthworks at the west end of Uffington Park (Fig.4), which are matched by corresponding ridges, mounds and hollows on the ground. Although the site was disrupted by the construction of Stamford Canal in the seventeenth century, certain geometric earthwork contours are suggestive of the foundations of buildings. These will be what Peck was referring to in the early-eighteenth century when he declared that there were no remains of either the church or priory apart from some

6

traces of the foundations and building just discernible above the ground (Peck (iii)). Since the canal was operational until as late as 1844, Peck would have been readily able to differentiate the remains of buildings and workings connected with the construction of the navigation from remnants of older structures associated with the priory. A more detailed analysis of the earthworks is attempted in Chapter 13.

Fig.4 Satellite image of the west end of Uffington Park (© 2018 Google/ Image © 2018 Getmapping plc)

Considering the enigmatic topography of the parkland and the importance of Uffington's erstwhile house of Augustinian canons, there is a surprising lack of awareness of the site's history. Neither the report of a detailed archaeological survey of Uffington Park in 1991, relating to a proposal to convert it to a golf course (Hall and Ford), nor South Kesteven District Council's review of the conservation area in 2015 (South Kesteven District Council), made any mention of there having been a priory in the vicinity.

Footnotes

1. Royal Commission on the Historical Monuments of England (UK)

2. An area of the west end of Uffington Park was formerly known as Horse Shoe Hurn (LAO [a]; Bunham and Arden). The origins and meaning of this name are obscure.

3. At the bottom left-hand corner of the brown, ploughed field in Fig.4, where the avenue ends abruptly at the canal

4. Presumed to be the same, or at least in the same position, as the bridge which stood in the twelfth century

5. Now the A1175

5. Augustinian Canons

When he founded Newstead, William de Albini III stipulated that the master of the house should be 'a priest and canon regular, a man of honest and approved religion' and that he should be assisted by a second resident canon, both of whom should live by the rule of Saint Augustine (Dugdale). The master and his assistant canon were to be aided in their duties by other ministers, later specified as a deacon and a clerk (Dugdale).

The Augustinian Canons (Canons Regular of St Augustine) were introduced into England in about 1100 (Cownie) and eventually became the most numerous religious order in the country (Dickinson [a] (iii)), with more houses than any other (Heale). The majority of their houses were small or medium-sized foundations. Regular canons were communities of clergy who lived together under a rule. They were priests and clerks (Franklin JA).

A CANNON REGVLAR OF St AVGVSTINE.

Vol. 2 P 1.

Fig.5   An Augustinian canon (Reproduced from *Monasticon Anglicanum*)

The Augustinian Canons were commonly known as Black Canons after their black cope and hood, which were worn over a fur almuce, a long wide-sleeved white linen rochet (or a surplice), and a fur-lined black cassock (Fig.5) (Clark; Dickinson [a] (iv)). They might also wear a black biretta (Webb) and their footwear was above-knee leather boots (Clark).

In choosing the Augustinians over the other orders with monasteries in Britain, de Albini was following the same path as many earlier Norman nobles drawn to the regular canons' combined values of monasticism and a duty of pastoral care to the populace. Houses were commonly established by wealthy barons or lords with the encouragement of a bishop (Heale), and thus William de Albini III would have been a typical patron.[1] He may have been seeking spiritual redemption after being excommunicated by Pope Innocent III in 1215 but potential practical advantages would have included hospitality at the priory, a secretariat providing clerical assistance with charters and other family records, care in infirmity or old age, and burial in a sacred location (Cownie). Patronage of a monastery was also a status symbol (Heale).

Footnotes

1. By the end of the twelfth century, foundation of an Augustinian house had also come within the reach of benefactors of more modest means and political power (Burton, Janet).

6. The Prior and Canons of Newstead by Stamford

The charter of William de Albini IV authorised the canons to elect their own prior (Dugdale), although the patron retained the right to issue a licence before an election could take place (Hill [a] (i)). The prior was concerned with the general governance of the house and maintenance of the monastic rule. As well as his spiritual and administrative duties, he was responsible for discipline, both assessing the punishment for offences and inflicting it himself (Clark).

Priors

A list of masters and priors of Newstead by Stamford is given in Table 1.

Name (with variations)	Date	Source	Notes
Walter *capellanus*	1224/5–	Smith & London (Davis FN [a]. Linc. Epis. Reg. Rolls of Wells, p.135)	chaplain first master
Adam of Herefeld	1225/6–	Smith & London (Davis FN [a]. Linc. Epis. Reg. Rolls of Wells, p.150)	canon of Missenden
Walter	1231/2–	Smith & London (Davis FN [a]. Linc. Epis. Reg. Rolls of Wells, p.202)	canon of Wilemerdel
Walter de Crek	1246–	Smith & London (Linc. Epis. Reg. Rolls of Grosseteste)	first recorded prior
Hamo of Greatford (Hamon; Gretford)	1263–85	Smith & London (Linc. Epis. Reg. Rolls of Gravesend)	
Peter de Berham (Barham)	1285–87	Smith & London (Reg. Sutton, I, pp.70-1)	d.1287
Thomas of Deeping (Deping)	1287–92	Smith & London (Reg. Sutton, I, pp.70-1)	resigned in 1292
Robert of Stamford (Staumford, Staunford)	1292–1308	Smith & London (Reg. Sutton, I, pp.70-1)	

Henry of Overton	1308–	Smith & London	
Geoffrey	occurs 1377, 1381	Smith DM	
William de Prestwold (Prestewolde)	occurs 1391	Smith DM	
William Sutton (Suttone)	occurs 1435, resigned 1436	Smith DM	
William Lylleforde (Lilleford)	occurs 1440	Smith DM	there is no record of the date of Lylleforde's election or institution
John Dankaster	not known	Simons	
Robert Exelby (Exilby)	died 1502	Smith DM (Eshelby HD)	also appointed prior of Fineshade in 1502 but died the same year
Stephen Sharpe (Sherp, Sherpe, Scharp, Scherp)	1502–24	Smith DM	
Thomas Hallam (Halam, Halame)	1524–34	Smith DM	acknowledged royal supremacy in July 1534
Philip Gawdeby	1534–	Smith DM	
Richard Lynne (Lyne)	occurs 1535	Smith DM	resigned by 30 Jan 1536
John Blakett (Blakytt, Blakytte, Blakyth, Blaky)	occurs 1536	Smith DM	the last prior

Table 1. Priors of Newstead by Stamford (Alternative versions of names shown in brackets)

Information about the heads of the house is patchy in some sources and vague or ambiguous in others. In a document registered in 1525 (LAO [b]), pertaining to the earliest days of Newstead's existence, the master identified with William de Albini and Agatha was Walter rather than Adam of Herefield (Franklin M J). If the transition from hospital to priory occurred between 1236 and 1242, this would be consistent with the incumbents appointed in 1226 and 1232 being masters. However, while the first recorded prior was Walter de Crek, who was elected in 1247 (Davis FN [b]), a charter dated 7 December 1239 refers explicitly to the prior and canons of Newstead rather than to the master and brothers (Historical Manuscripts Commission (ii)), which points to there having been at least one other prior before him.

The date of Sutton's election as prior is not known. There is no record either of the date of Lylleforde's election or institution but it may not have occurred immediately after Sutton's resignation since there were no other religious personnel remaining at Newstead Priory at that time (Thompson [a]). The list of priors is undoubtedly incomplete given that only about twenty names are known for a period of more than 300 years and some incumbents, such as Peter de Berham and Philip Gawdeby, had very brief tenures. Gaps in the record are most likely between Henry of Overton and Geoffrey, William de Prestwold and William Sutton, and William Lylleforde and Robert Exelby. Legal records from the reign[1] of Edward IV show that John Dankaster, prior of Newstead by the Bridge of the Wass between Uffington and Stamford, was sued by John Belvoir, prior of the church of Blessed Mary, for non-payment of a debt (Simons) but his term of office is unknown.[2] The two longest-known tenures were those of Hamo of Greatford and Stephen Sharpe, who each served for 22 years.

There is some disagreement as to the identity of the last prior. Although Bishop John Longland wrote to Thomas Cromwell recommending John Blakytt, 'a right honest sobre man', for the vacant position following the resignation of the previous incumbent (Wright), and Page states that John Blaky was the last prior of Newstead by Stamford (Page [a]), both the *Valor Ecclesiasticus* and *Monasticon Anglicanum* (Dugdale) record that it was Richard Lynne who has this distinction. Notwithstanding this, and although it has been mooted that Longland's recommendation was ignored (Wright), the deed granting the remains and site of the priory to Richard Manners in 1538/9 named John Blakett as the last prior (LAO [c]).[3]

Newly-elected priors were presented to the bishop of Lincoln for admission. On occasions, the bishop used his power of veto to declare elections null and void. In 1285 Bishop Sutton countermanded the election of Robert of Stamford, in succession to Hamo, on the grounds of extreme irregularity in the procedures and took it upon himself to appoint Peter of Barham instead (Hill [a] (ii)). Following the resignation of Thomas of Deeping in 1292, the bishop again declared Robert of Stamford's election invalid on procedural grounds but then instituted him upon his own responsibility (Hill [a] (iii)). In doing so he may have been pointedly asserting his ultimate authority over the affairs of the priory.

Canons

Having found no evidence of any canons other than the prior and confrater in the early years of the house, Stamford antiquary Francis Peck questioned whether the deacon and clerk appointed to assist them in divine service, in compliance with the second charter of William de Albini III, were any more than minor canons at most (Peck (iii)). He deduced from William de Albini IV's concession allowing the canons to elect their own prior that the complement of canons had increased by that time.

The number of canons at Newstead fluctuated but there were probably never more than seven (Franklin MJ). There were seven in 1377, five in 1381, five in 1440, four in 1534 and four in 1536 (Knowles and Hadcock). It appears that there were no canons for a time after Prior Sutton resigned in 1435 (Thompson [a]) but the number had recovered to five by 1440 (Thompson [b]). In 1525 there were three canons in addition to the prior (Thompson [c]). When Bishop Longland wrote to Cromwell in January 1536 there were only two canons remaining (Wright) but the number had risen again to four, including a new prior and a novice, by the time the house was dissolved later that year (Page [a]). With such small numbers, the priory struggled to fulfil its obligations. Shortly before the end, a tenant who was being sued for not paying a particular rent argued that the original bequest required that the canons should sing for the soul of Walter Huntingfield but that they had failed to allocate a priest for this purpose for many years because there were so few of them (Page [a]).

Footnotes

1. 1461–70 and 1471–83

2. In another case concerning an unpaid debt (image 540), John Stamford, prior of the Blessed Mary, sued Thomas Baroughby, a clerk of Stook by Grantham (Simons), but in this instance it is uncertain whether the location of the Newstead priory was Sherwood or Uffington; John Stamford's name does not appear on the list of priors of Newstead Abbey in *Monasticon Anglicanum.*

3. Confusion could potentially have arisen by dint of the fact that the last prior (or abbot) of Newstead Abbey (De Novo Loco in Sherwood) was called John Blake (Page [b]).

7. Life in the Priory

Newstead's poor and infirm residents were chosen from William de Albini III's own tenants, or from others, as agreed by him in consultation with the prior and confrater (Peck (ii)).

In following the Rule of St Augustine, the Newstead canons were bound by vows of obedience, poverty and chastity and they observed the seven canonical hours and the ecclesiastical fasts (Webb). Their daily prayers were comparatively short and simple (Dickinson [a] (iv)). Individual houses of Augustinian canons operated largely independently of one another (Heale) but, while very little is known with certainty about the internal affairs of Newstead by Stamford (Wood), some generalisations can be made (Gasquet). Menial duties would have been carried out by paid servants and there may also have been lay brothers (Webb)[1], chosen for their proficiency in a craft likely to be useful to the house (Coppack). This would have freed the canons to devote their day to prayer, study, education, charity, hospitality and other good works (Webb). Scholarly, artistic and creative pursuits may have included preparing parchment, writing, illuminating and binding books, scoring music, carving and painting, making and repairing their own garments, and fashioning baskets and mats (Webb; Dickinson [a] (v)). The Newstead canons kept an unusual book which recorded not only their monastery's own estate and endowments but all of the estates and possessions of the neighbourhood in and around Stamford. Regrettably, this invaluable record was destroyed or lost at the Dissolution (Peck (iii)). Outdoors, the canons may have cultivated the gardens and worked in the fields (Dickinson [a] (v)). Silence would have been observed in the church, refectory and dormitory except where muted speech was deemed necessary (Dickinson [a] (vi)), such as during the daily gathering in the chapter house (Burton, Janet).

Nothing is known specifically about the servants at Newstead but the regular workforce would have included domestic staff, agricultural labourers and construction workers.

When numbers allowed, the canons would have been allocated managerial roles, such as sacrist, infirmarer, chamberlain, cellarer and refector, although some offices may of necessity have been combined or possibly been assigned to lay brothers. The sacrist was in charge of the monastic church and of everything required for conducting the services. Amongst his other duties, the chamberlain procured and maintained the canons' clothes (Webb). In the early years of Newstead's existence, the master's livery and shoe money was taken from the general income of the hospital, whereas the two canons living with him received one mark from the rent of Ralph Wake of Chalfont for this purpose (LAO [b]). The latter rent also paid for the livery and shoes of the residents. Later, given the predilection of black canons for good quality cloth (Knowles [a] (i)), the chamberlain may have sourced Stamford's high-quality woven woollen cloth, haberget, for the canons' habits. Besides caring for sick brethren, the infirmarer would have performed bloodletting on the canons at regulated intervals throughout the year (Webb), a practice believed to provide protection against disease (Clark). The cellarer organised the supply of foodstuffs and other general supplies, while the refector was responsible for running the kitchen and providing meals, with which he would have been assisted by a staff of secular cooks and workers (Frost). In the beginning, each resident received a daily loaf made with salted or sieved flour and sprinkled with spice, and they shared five gallons of ale every day (LAO [b]). Lunch comprised a dish of meat, whereas dinner was determined by what the house could afford. During Lent each pair of residents received five herrings or six eggs daily along with their drinks allowance. If an individual was particularly unwell a more suitable menu could be substituted by the infirmarer with the master's consent (LAO [b]). The canons would have eaten two wholesome meals per day, comprising fish, meat and vegetables, washed down with beer (Webb). They would consume more beer before retiring to bed. Much of the food came from the de Albini household and from the priory's lands. As well as granting fishing rights in the Gwash, Isabel de Ros pledged a regular supply of beer from her tenants (Willis, F E d'A).

Regular canons were immediately answerable to their diocesan bishop (Franklin JA). Their monasteries were frequently endowed with parish churches (Heale) and, in some instances, canons in holy orders would conduct services and undertake parochial duties in the impropriated churches (Gasquet). The nature of the relationship between the Newstead canons and the parish church of St Michael and All Angels, less than a mile distant in Uffington village, is uncertain but, as the church was mostly in the patronage of Belvoir Priory (Historical Manuscripts Commission (i)), it is unlikely that the canons provided ministerial and pastoral services to it.

Newstead by Stamford was instituting clergy to benefices in the archdeaconries of Lincoln (Hill [a] (iv)) and Northampton (Hill [b]) by at least 1280 (Hill [a] (iv)). However, the priory did not always conduct its affairs by the book. In May 1282 William de Helingeye was appointed to the benefice of the church of Saint Michael Major at Stamford but this was challenged a year later by the patron, the Abbot and Convent of Crowland, who presented an alternative candidate on the grounds that the incumbent had not taken major orders and that he was not resident at the time (Hill [a] (v)).

During the decade 1290–99, Newstead by Stamford recorded only nine ordinations of fraters but granted seventy-seven titles (Hill [c]). A bishop was permitted to ordain an ordinand to holy orders only if he was prepared to keep the new priest at his own expense or was satisfied that the candidate for ordination had visible means of support, known as a 'title', by which he could be suitably maintained until he found paid employment (Hill [c]). One of the ways that a title could be obtained was through membership of a religious order—an individual house of regular canons had an obligation to make corporate provision for the support of its members. Most likely, Newstead will have granted the seventy-seven titles in question to secular clerics as a means of external accreditation by which the house confirmed their eligibility to be consecrated to holy orders (Swanson, personal communication). Rather than providing financial support in these circumstances, the priory might even have charged a small fee for certifying that the recipients were suitably qualified and had independent financial resources.[2]

Newstead's priors played an important role in secular life. As well as making religious appointments, disciplining errant clerics and initiating excommunications (Hill [d]), the prior's court dispensed legal judgements, including hearing and settling lawsuits, granting probate of wills (Hill [e] (i)), and arbitrating in disputes (Hill [f] (i)). In turn, Newstead issued similar commissions to leaders of other religious houses (Hill [e] (ii); [f] (ii)). In the mid-thirteenth century, priors were frequently engaged as itinerant justices, although this was deprecated by Bishop Grosseteste (Knowles [b] (i)).

Governance of the priory was monitored by regular visits from the diocesan bishop and representatives nominated by the Augustinian congregation, each of whom had their own independent scheme of visitation.

Footnotes

1. In smaller monasteries many of the routine jobs and housekeeping may have been done by the religious themselves.

2. Many titles were granted by relatively small and poor houses and the number of titles granted was often inversely related to the wealth of the house. This practice may simply have been a bureaucratic exercise to confirm that the candidate met the criteria for ordination and which did not obligate the house to provide financial support to the recipient of the title. Possibly it was a means of generating a modest income, although there is no known evidence for this from account rolls (Swanson, personal communication).

8. General Chapters and Visitations

The Lateran Council of 1215 decreed that religious orders should hold general chapters every three years, at which the heads of each house (or their representatives) would convene to draw up statutes about the reform of the order and the observance of the Rule. During the following year, the heads of the Augustinian monasteries in the two provinces of Canterbury and York met at Leicester (Salter HE). The northern and southern provinces of black canons separated sometime after 1220 or 1223, each to hold its own triennial chapter, until Pope Benedict XII ruled in 1339 that they were to reunite. On 12 March 1341 the new series of gatherings commenced with a chapter at Newstead by Stamford, and in 1353 the meeting at Oseney decided that future chapters should be held alternately at Newstead and Northampton. Further general chapters were held at Newstead by Stamford in 1356, 1362, 1371, 1377 and 1383. One of the three new statutes passed in 1371 was that St Augustine should be mentioned in the Confiteor. Peck may have had a reputation for hyperbole but he might not have been far from the truth when he spoke of 'the flourishing monastery of Newstede' (Peck (iii)), at least in relation to this period of its history.

Reputed to be a small house, it may at first seem surprising that Newstead was chosen as a regular venue for the triennial general chapter in the mid-fourteenth century. However, Stamford was a large and thriving town with a strong religious tradition (Sheehan [c] (i)) and when the northern and southern provinces of the order were reunited it was expedient to hold the chapters at a house near the boundary of the two provinces, such as Newstead by Stamford, Northampton or Leicester (Knowles [b] (ii)). With both the main north–south Roman road Ermine Street (and the Great North Road that later superseded it in importance) and the River Welland both passing through the middle of Stamford, transport links via road and river were good and there would have been ample accommodation in the town for members attending convocations. Little is known about the priors during this purple patch.

Education was an important element of Augustinian life. From 1334 heads of houses were required to provide lecturers to teach the canons and to assign a time and a place for such teaching (Orme). Pope Benedict XII issued legislation in 1339 requiring each monastery to maintain a schoolmaster to instruct the canons in the 'primitive sciences' of grammar, logic and philosophy (Orme). In 1356 the general chapter at Newstead by Stamford decreed that Augustinian houses should send scholars to the universities (which in Britain at that time existed only at Oxford and Cambridge (Sheehan [c] (ii))), where they would be under the jurisdiction of a prior studentium.[1] Because the pope's edict applied only to houses with a minimum of twenty members, Newstead itself would have been exempt by virtue of its small size.

Representatives were appointed from among the delegates attending general chapters, whose remit it was to conduct regular visitations to each house of the order for the purpose of ensuring observance of the Rule and compliance with the statutes.

Footnotes

1. This was the first time that the prior studentium of the Augustinians was mentioned at any chapter.

9. Episcopal Visits

As well as visitations by officials of their own order appointed by the provincial or general chapter, all Augustinian houses were visited regularly by their diocesan bishop (Webb). Although they both essentially performed the same task, they normally did so independently of one another. Visitations were aimed at maintaining standards (Hoskin). The bishop's responsibilities included monitoring discipline and behaviour, with a view to eradicating dissent, misconduct and corruption.

Ideally, the whole diocese should have been visited once every three years but, because the diocese of Lincoln covered an area bounded by the River Humber in the North and the Thames in the South, such a target was well-nigh impossible to achieve (Hill [g]). There is no record of Bishop Robert Grosseteste having visited Newstead by Stamford during his 18-year term of office between 1235 and 1253 (Hoskin).

During his episcopate from 1280 to 1299, Bishop Oliver Sutton travelled almost continuously when not attending meetings of parliament or convocation, or during his rare periods of illness. Normally he would base his activities on one of his castles or manor houses but at other times he would remain for several days at one of the wealthier religious houses of the diocese, including Newstead by Stamford (Hill [g]).

Newstead was visited by John Dalderby, Bishop of Lincoln, in 1301, 1304, 1306 and 1309 (Clubley; Peck (iv)), Bishop John Gynwell of Lincoln in 1348 (Willis, F E d'A), Bishop William of Alnwick in 1440 (Thompson [b]), and Bishop John Longland of Lincoln in 1525 (Thompson [c]).

When Bishop Alnwick visited on 21 October 1440, there appear to have been five canons, including William Lylleforde, the prior (Thompson [b]). However, one of the five, John Depyng, was living at Ulverscroft Priory in Leicestershire with the prior's permission, and another, whose name was not recorded, was seriously ill and too sick to appear. A fourth canon, John Polvertofte, had transferred to Newstead from Fineshade Priory. The fifth was called Spaldyng. Lylleforde complained that the house was 20 marks in debt and almost in ruins through the improvidence of his predecessor, Sutton. It had been five pounds in debt at the time of his installation. Informed by Brother Spaldyng that they no longer rose at night to sing Matins because they were so few in number, the bishop instructed that they should get up every night to recite them even if they could not be sung. He also ordered that Brother Depyng be brought back from Ulverscroft Priory without delay.

At Bishop Longland's visit on 20 May 1525, all was reported well with the prior and three canons. The prior was Thomas Hallam and the canons were Edward Merston, Phillip Gawdeby and Robert Cokerell (Thompson [c]).[1]

Footnotes

1. A decade later Phillip Gawdeby would briefly succeed Thomas Hallam as prior.

10. Relationship between the Priories of Newstead and Belvoir

The relationship between Newstead Priory and Belvoir Priory is enigmatic. As Lord of Uffington and Belvoir, William de Albini III will have felt a loyalty to both houses, although Newstead, being his personal foundation, will surely have taken precedence. Whereas Newstead was an Augustinian house, Belvoir was a cell of St Albans Abbey, a Benedictine institution (Sheehan [b] (i)). Newstead did not have a mother house.

Despite his closer connections with Newstead, in about the year 1230 de Albini gave the advowson of the church of Redmile to the monks of Belvoir (Caley, Ellis and Bandinel).[1] Long before the hospital was founded at Newstead, the advowson and parsonage of Uffington Church had been granted to Belvoir Priory by Cecily de Belvoir (d.1168) (Historic Manuscripts Commission (i)). William de Albini III, who was her grandson, ratified this gift, and Pope Alexander III confirmed it in 1177 (Historic Manuscripts Commission (i)). The advowson was later held (or claimed) by William de Ros of Hamlake[2] (a descendant of William de Albini III), who in 1322 gave the prior of Belvoir, John de Kendale, and the convent permission to purchase the church for their own use (Historical Manuscripts Commission (ii)). In 1364 prior William and the convent of Belvoir presented Robert de Tylton, a clerk to Thomas de Ros, to Uffington Church following the death of the previous incumbent, William de Houghton.[3] Thomas de Ros[4] emphasised that this should not prejudice the priory and that the prior and convent should present to that church in accordance with the charter of Lady Cecily Bigod; he too consented to the priory acquiring the church for their own use if they were able to (Historical Manuscripts Commission (i)). Thereafter, the prior and convent of Belvoir were the patron of Uffington Church continuously until the Dissolution.[5]

Although it had financial difficulties of its own (Page [d]), Belvoir Priory was evidently sympathetic to Newstead's poverty. Master John de Hada remitted small tithes on Newstead's lands at Uffington (Historical Manuscripts Commission (ii)) before he was instituted as rector of Uffington in 1238 (Hoskin)[6]. Prior William[7] and the convent confirmed his charter in another dated 7 December 1239, which also exempted Newstead from giving all tithes from their wind and water mills within the parish. In further concessions, Newstead was absolved from paying a mortuary[8], or anything else, to Uffington Church in the event of a servant dying at the priory. Its servants were permitted to receive all the sacraments at the priory (with the exception of confession and marriage unless the pope or the bishop of Lincoln should give them a dispensation to do so) (Historical Manuscripts Commission (ii)). In return, the Newstead canons were to pay the rector half a mark[9] of silver a year. In 1273, in recompense for the continuing waiver of the tithes due from their house to Uffington Church, Prior Hamo and the convent of Newstead pledged to pay 20s. a year to the sacristan of Belvoir Priory for the ornaments and lights of the priory church until such time as a fixed rent of 20s. was assigned for the purpose (Historical Manuscripts Commission (ii)). It was still paying 20s. to the prior of Belvoir in 1526 (Salter H). Newstead's canons had financial obligations to Belvoir Priory at other times as well. In 1406 the prior and convent were bound to pay the prior and convent of Belvoir 40 pounds of English money come the following Midsummer, under penalty of distraint by an ecclesiastical or a secular judge (Historical Manuscripts Commission (ii)).

Notwithstanding its links with Belvoir through its founder, Newstead appears to have had a closer working relationship with the nearby Augustinian priories of Fineshade in Northamptonshire and Ulverscroft in Leicestershire, with which it exchanged canons (Thompson [b]).

Footnotes

1. This might imply that Newstead did not yet exist at that time.

2. William de Ros (d.1343), 2nd Baron de Ros

3. These names are shown as Robert de Tynton and William de Hogkton on the list of rectors in St Michael and All Angels Church in Uffington.

4. Thomas, 4th Baron de Ros {1336–84}

5. According to the board in Uffington Church

6. His name is shown as John de Lada in Uffington Church; it appears twice in succession with institution dates of 1231 and 1238. The reason for this is not apparent but the second date is consistent with his presentation by Belvoir Priory.

7. This will have been William of Huntingdon who was lately prior of Belvoir when John de Hada died in 1278 and was succeeded as Uffington rector by Nicholas de Ros (Page [d]).

8. A customary gift due to the incumbent of a parish in England from the estate of a deceased parishioner

9. 4 oz.

11. Financial Affairs of Newstead by Stamford

Although the priory prospered periodically, it can never have been rich. When Belvoir Priory agreed to remit the small tithe due from Newstead's prior and canons in 1239, just three years after the death of their founder, the reason given for this largesse was 'especially because they are in need' (Willis, F E d'A). Nevertheless, while it initially struggled financially following de Albini's death, by the late-thirteenth century Newstead by Stamford was deemed to be one of the wealthier religious houses in the Lincolnshire diocese (Hill [g]). The wealth of a house was based on a combination of temporal and spiritual incomes.

Temporalities were the most important component of the Augustinian economy. The major element was land, which the canons secured both by various forms of gift and through their own efforts of purchase and rental (Robinson [a]). A grant or gift to a monastery frequently came with conditions attached, such as an obligation to pray for the souls of the donor and his family and friends, the rite of burial in the priory church, or a commitment to maintain a memorial lamp or candle for the donor or benefactor (Robinson [a]).

No matter how diligent and efficient Newstead's clerks may have been in documenting its grants, gifts and agreements, it is unsurprising that a dispute sometimes arose over the ownership of a piece of land, resulting in a lawsuit being brought before the royal courts. In 1276 Prior Hamon, the tenant, acknowledged that a rent of 24s. payable on land in Uffington was the right of Maud de Gersindone; in return, Maud and her husband, Hugh, conditionally granted the rent to the prior and the Newstead church in perpetuity, for which the prior gave them 2 marks of silver (Medieval Genealogy).

When the temporalities of the clergy were assessed for the *Taxatio Eccesiastica* in 1291–92 at the behest of Pope Nicholas IV, the prior of Newstead without Stamford had £38.9s.5d. (*Taxatio*) (Table 2).[1]

Deanery	Temporality
Staunford (Stamford)	£9.3s.0d
Belteslawe (Beltisloe)	£1.4s.0d
Rotelund (Rutland)	£5.19s.11d
Corynghill (Collingham)	£10.0s.0d
Nesso (Ness)	£12.2s.6d

total £38.9s.5d.

Table 2. Temporalities of Newstead by Stamford Priory in 1292

The temporalities in Stamford Deanery comprised property in Stamford valued at £9.3s.0d. (Hartley and Rogers). Houses purchased in the parish of St John the Baptist in the mid-thirteenth century were worth 100s. annually (Roffe (i)). A house near the south-eastern end of Broad Street probably came by gift to the priory in 1359 (Hartley and Rogers). There was a house in St Mary's parish (Hartley and Rogers) and another in the parish of St Michael Cornstall, south of the town wall (Peck (v)). These properties would either have been retained by the priory for its own use or rented to tenants (Burton, Janet). An undated deed from the thirteenth or fourteenth century granted Newstead Priory the annual rent charge of 5s. from a house in All Saints parish in Stamford (Rogers (i)).

In addition to urban properties, temporal income was derived through ownership of arable land, meadows, pastures, stock, mills, fisheries and woods (Robinson [a]). Most of their order's land and property was amassed by the Augustinian canons by the end of the thirteenth century but additions were made throughout the Middle Ages (Robinson [a]).

Monastic life was highly dependent on the ownership of arable lands for the production of crops, chiefly grain, and pasture and meadow for the rearing of stock, principally sheep. When the Augustinian order contributed to the wool trade of England and Wales in the thirteenth and fourteenth centuries (Robinson [a]), Newstead would have been in a favourable position to capitalise on the popularity of the high-quality long fleeces of the local sheep, which were woven in Stamford into luxury cloth, such as haberget, or sent for export.

Newstead's income would also have derived from its mills, the sale of natural resources such as wood, and from its fishery. Water mills were a lucrative source of revenue (Coppack) and, in addition to its own mill at Uffington, the prior and canons rented Kingsmill outside Stamford on a permanent lease (Rogers (ii)).

The inquisition of 1274/75 for the Hundred Rolls was told that the prior of Newstead outside Stamford had appropriated to himself the free fishery in the River Gwash, from the River Welland to Smalebrigges, to the financial detriment of the town of Stamford (Roffe (ii)). Denial of the right of the wider community of the town to fish freely in the river at all times was contradictorily said to have cost Stamford either 2s. or 3s. a year over the preceding five years (Roffe (ii)). If, as a consequence, Newstead was made to forfeit this valuable benefit, it would be restored officially in 1298 when Isabel de Ros granted to the priory the right of fishing in the Gwash from Ryhall meadow to the Welland (Willis, F E d'A).

The prior held a manor in Little Casterton during the reign of King Edward II (Peck (vi); Page [e]). Possibly this originated from a grant to the prior in 1278 by Hugh, son of Hugh de Welledon, and Joan, his wife, of four messuages, a mill, a toft, 6½ virgates and 8½ acres of land, and 8s. rent in Little Casterton, in return for newly-built accommodation in the priory court, fuel, access to church services, lifelong daily allowances of meat or fish, bread and ale, and hay, straw and grass for a sheep and a cow. In 1509 Stephen Scharp, prior of Newstead, granted lands in Little Casterton to Christopher Browne of Tolethorpe and in 1534 Prior Thomas Halam granted lands there to Christopher Buckingham (Page [e]).

Manors were a major economic asset since the canons would benefit threefold from the service owed to the demesne by tenants, rent for the tenanted land, and the profits of manorial courts (Burton, Janet; Robinson [a]). The late arrival of the Augustinian order in England meant that the gift of manors was comparatively rare. Houses wishing to control manorial holdings had largely to create them artificially, building them up piecemeal through gift and purchase (Robinson [a]). Newstead by Stamford eventually possessed manors and other lands over a wide area in Lincolnshire, Northamptonshire and Rutland (Rogers (iii)), including lands in the village or fields of Braunston in Northants (Page [f]).

Another source of temporal income was the knight's fee.[2] In 1242–43 the prior of Newstead held half a fee in Braunteston (Braunston) from Oliver de Eyncurt[3] (*Liber Feodorum* (i)). Concurrent with this, the prior had from William de Albini one half of a knight's fee in Uffington and Tallington from a new feoffment (*Liber Feodorum* (ii)). In 1303 he held a twelfth of a knight's fee in Uffington, Tallington and Casewick (*Feudal Aids* (i)), which had increased to a quarter of a fee in 1346 (with the exception of a part held by Peter de Ros) (*Feudal Aids* (ii)). Newstead also benefited from other donations and bequests. In 1424 Roger Flower of Oakham left to the prior and canons a legacy of 13s.4d. (Peck (vii)) and in 1530 Edward Watson of Lyddington in Rutland left them 10s. in his will (Foster).

Seemingly only a small part of Newstead's income derived from spiritualities in the form of churches, rectories, tithes, oblations, other voluntary offerings and payments such as burial dues.[4] In 1301 Isabel granted to the priory the advowson of Stoke Albany in Northamptonshire and in 1308 her son William de Ros gave a share in the advowson of Grayingham in Lincolnshire (Page [a]).[5] The benefice of a parish church was the major constituent of Augustinian spiritual revenue and its largest component by far was the tithes (Robinson [a]). The advowson empowered the prior and convent to present a chaplain or clerk for the position of rector and then to receive a fixed annual pension based on the total income of the benefice. If the advowson was shared, then so were these rights. Although Newstead's prior and canons presented to the church of Little Casterton in Rutland in 1283[6], its right to do so appears to have been disputed in that Sir John de Oketon and his wife, Alice, presented William de Empingham to the same church within three months (Page [e]). The Little Casterton advowson was reputedly held by the priory in 1321 (Page [a]) when Henry le Scrope purchased it and obtained licence to alienate it to the prior of Newstead in exchange for all the lands that the prior held in Little Casterton (Page[e]). However, the actual position is uncertain because Empingham is said to have retained the living until his death in 1331 and Scrope himself presented to the church during that year and was still in possession of the advowson when he died in 1336 (Page [e]). Appropriation of a church to a monastery was much more valuable than an advowson because the convent became its rector and received all of its revenue (Robinson [a]). In this event it normally delegated the duty of the cure of the souls to a priest and paid him a proportion of the total income of the benefice. There is no record of Newstead ever having had any appropriated churches. Considering that tithes were by far the chief form of spiritual income for the Augustinian order in general (Robinson [a]), the Uffington house appears to have missed out badly in this respect.

The financial outgoings of the priory would have incorporated the costs associated with conducting the business of the house, feeding and clothing the canons and residents, building and maintenance, the prior's allowance, wages for servants and hired labour, hospitality, accommodation and stabling for visitors and their servants, alms, charitable donations and taxes.

Houses of Augustinian canons founded after the turn of the thirteenth century by local nobility were particularly liable to economic as well as moral instability (Dickinson [a] (vii)). Despite the munificence of the de Albinis and the assorted benefactions of others, Newstead by Stamford gradually fell into poverty. While mismanagement and prodigality may have contributed to its debts, some of the factors conducing to the financial plight of the house may have been beyond the prior's control. Because a small but significant part of its annual revenue would have been dependent on income from its churches and parishioners' tithes, this element would have been vulnerable to fluctuations in the size of the population of the parish and would rise and fall proportionately (Heale). Table 3 shows the estimated population of Uffington parish over a period spanning the lifetime of the priory.

Date	Population (estimated)	Households	Source
1086	225	50	Domesday Survey
1332	234/300	52	Taxpayers' returns
1563	200/233	53	Archdeacon's return to Bishop

Table 3. Uffington population (Extracted from Sheehan [b] (ii))

Although the local population appears from these figures to have been remarkably stable during this period of almost 500 years, the general dearth of information may hide considerable fluctuations in the fourteenth and fifteenth centuries. Like that of many other houses of Augustinian canons, Newstead's income would certainly have been seriously impacted by the Black Death in 1348–49 and subsequent further outbreaks of plague, when the population of England fell by around 40 per cent and remained stagnant for the next 150 years (Heale).

Over time, Newstead by Stamford slid into financial and spiritual decline. Its buildings were in virtual ruins by 1427 (Willis, F E d'A). Alas, its poverty did not exempt it from punitive taxation.

In 1523, at the behest of Lord Chancellor Thomas Wolsey, heavy taxes were imposed to subsidise Henry VIII's grandiose foreign policy. A new valuation was made of religious houses and a percentage of one year's revenue of the house was required to be paid to the Exchequer in instalments over five years. The rate of payment varied according to circumstances and, when income was estimated, certain deductions were allowed (Salter H). In 1526 the combined spiritualities and temporalities of the prior and convent of Newstead by Stamford amounted to £57.6s. Allowable deductions included a pension of £5.13s.4d. to Prior Stephen Sharpe, 6s.8d. to the rector of Uffington, 5s. to the pope, 12d. to the king, various payments to the heads of other religious houses, and the cost of repairs. The allowances totalled £12.13s.11d., meaning that the sum upon which the subsidy was payable was £44.12s.1d. Stephen Sharpe paid a subsidy of 7s.6d. on his pension, roughly equating to a rate of one fifteenth.

An additional tax burden was avoided in 1525 when the supposedly voluntary 'Amicable Grant', proclaimed by Cardinal Wolsey without parliamentary approval, was revoked by the king in the face of strong popular opposition. It would have overlapped with the collection of the 1523 subsidy and required clergy to pay a levy of one third on their belongings (Fletcher and MacCulloch).

Bishop Longland referred to Newstead's poverty in his letter to Cromwell in the final days of the priory (Wright). The yearly revenue of Newstead at the Dissolution has been variously stated as £37.6s.0d. or £42.1s.3d. (Peck (viii); Drakard; Burton, Geo; Harrod; Howgrave). The lower figure indicates the net income of the house after deduction of allowable expenses of £4.15s.3d. (*Valor*), including £2.4s.8d. in respect of compulsory alms (Savine). According to the *Valor Ecclesiasticus*, as well as its demesne and its property in Stamford, Newstead had lands, tenements or rents assessed at over £5 in Braunston and Little Casterton and nine others elsewhere assessed at under £5 (Robinson [b]). None of the priory's revenue at that time was accounted for by spiritualities (Robinson [b]).

Although more accurate and comprehensive than the *Taxatio* (Robinson [a]), for the country as a whole the *Valor* underestimated monastic income by as much as 15 per cent, or even more (Knowles [a] (i)). A subsequent valuation of the monasteries conducted by the suppression commissioners in early 1536 registered a marked increase in net annual income when compared to the returns of the commissioners of the tenth the previous year (Knowles [a] (ii)).[7] In Lincolnshire the assessed values exceeded those of the *Valor* by an average of 41.9 per cent (Robinson[a]). By comparison with the net value of £37.6s.0d. recorded in the *Valor*, Newstead's value according to the Ministers' Accounts was £43.8s.1d. (Table 4), a considerably smaller proportional difference than for Lincolnshire houses in general.

Its revenue at the Dissolution put Newstead by Stamford in the second smallest of five divisions of monastic houses, as defined by an income of between £20 and £100; this group constituted 35 per cent of the total (Knowles [a] (i)). That none of this income was accounted for by spiritualities (Nichols) indicates that Newstead had lost all of its churches by then. Howgrave put these sums into context by citing inflation with reference to the wages of a haymaker. In the reign of Henry VII they were one penny a day and they did not exceed three half pence in the reign of Henry VIII, whereas they were twelve pence per day by the first quarter of the eighteenth century (Howgrave). It is clear that, by the time of its demise, Newstead Priory had been reduced to penury, both financially and ecclesiastically, stripped of most of its wealth, power and influence.

Comput' Ministrorum Domini Regis *temp.* Hen. VIII.

[Abstract of Roll, 28 Hen. VIII. Augmentation Office.]

Prioratus de Newsted.

Com' Linc'	£. s. d.
Bramston–Redd' assis' lib' ten'	0 12 8
Bramston–Redd' ten'	14 0 6
Northton	
Dadyngton–Terr' arabil', &c.	0 15 0
Rutland	
Ketton—Prat' et terr'	2 0 0
Linc'	
Stanford—Firma ten'	1 2 0
Grayngham—Mess' et terr', &c.	4 10 0
Botylford—Firma ten'	0 5 0
Colsterworth—Terr' prat' et pastur'	0 8 0
Caswyhe—Firma claus'	2 0 0
Offynton—Firma toft', terr', &c.	0 13 4
Casterton Parva—Ten' prat' et pastur'	5 0 0
Stamford—Terr' ten', &c.	4 8 8
Newsted—Terr' dnical'	7 12 11

(total £43.8s.1d.)

Table 4. Annual Revenue of Newsted juxta Stamford at the Dissolution - Ministers' Accounts (Dugdale)

Footnotes

1. An alternative figure of £38.16s.11d is given in Peck's *Annals* owing to different sums being recorded for Beltisloe and Ness (Peck (ix)). Robinson quotes a figure of £42.2s.9d (Robinson [b]). Regardless of these discrepancies, the *Taxatio Ecclesiastica* probably greatly underestimated the true values of ecclesiastical income (Robinson [a]).

2. A unit measure of land sufficient to support one knight in the performance of his feudal duties

3. Alternatively, Dayncurt

4. For the order as a whole, a greater proportion of the wealth of Augustinian houses derived from temporalities than from spiritualities, in a ratio of 2:1 in 1535 (Robinson [a]).

5. Parish churches were often divided into two (moieties) or even three (portions) benefices (Robinson [a]).

6. 1281 according to Peck (Peck (x))

7. The Act of March 1536, which provided for the suppression of the lesser monasteries, was accompanied by another establishing The Court of Augmentations (Knowles [a] (iii)) whose function it was to administer monastic properties and revenues confiscated by the Crown.

12. Dissolution

It is evident that the priory had no inkling of the impending cataclysm in the Church when in 1525 prior Thomas Hallam took out an 80-year lease on a parcel of ground outside Stamford, between the town walls and the River Welland, at a rent of 12d. per annum (Rogers (iv)). As one of the smaller religious houses with an annual income of less than £200, Newstead was dissolved in the first wave of suppressions in 1536. Its dissolution occurred after 7 August 1536 (Jack).

When the end came, only the prior, two canons and a novice remained (Page [a]). Statutory provision was made for the community of doomed houses (Knowles [a] (iv)). Newstead's prior received a pension of £15 (Page [a]), while the options open to the canons would have been to transfer to a surviving Augustinian house or to relinquish their vows and pursue a secular career (Knowles [a] (iv)). The liquidation of the priory may not have been an entirely unwelcome setback for the canons since across the country almost half of all Augustinian canons had expressed a wish to be released from their vows of poverty and obedience and leave the religious life—the proportion was even higher in the smaller houses of the congregation (Knowles [a] (ii)). If they were in holy orders, one option was to become a secular priest and apply for an ecclesiastical benefice or chaplaincy (Knowles [a] (iv)). Otherwise, they might have sought clerical employment. Servants and farmhands would either have been paid off by the royal commissioners or been kept on by the subsequent lay owner or tenant. There being less of an immediate demand for redundant domestic servants, there may have been a flood of cooks, bakers, brewers, dairy maids, cleaners, porters and others into the local labour market.

Although no reports of their visitations survive for houses in Lincolnshire (and hence for Newstead by Stamford) (Knowles [a] (ii); (v)), once the fate of a monastery was sealed, the suppression commissioners will soon have returned to dismiss the community, sell the livestock and personal possessions, despatch the plate and jewels to London, and dismantle the buildings or hand them over to the farmer or grantee (Knowles [a] (ii)). The transfer of plate and jewels to the royal treasury would have been followed by the sale of the church and domestic furniture, with the chapterhouse or cloister possibly becoming the auction room for on-the-spot sales (Knowles [a] (vi)). Everything that could be priced was put up for sale, from building materials such as bricks, tiles and paving stones to ecclesiastical trappings such as vestments, missals, candlesticks, censers, pulpits and organs, many of them to be put to uses very different from their original purpose. The bells and the leaden roofs of the churches, halls and barns were particularly valuable and, whenever possible, furnaces were set up alongside and the metal melted into pigs (Knowles [a] (vi)). Newstead's bells, roofing lead and other high value items such as altar plate were worth only £12.18s. (Page [a]).

There may have been little reason to retain Newstead's old priory buildings. Except where an alternative use could be identified for them, the official policy was that the commissioners, or the new owner, should 'pull down to the ground all the walls of the churches, stepulls, cloysters, fraterys, dorters, chapter howsys' and the rest (Knowles [a] (vi)). However, because of the high cost of demolition, active destruction was frequently less radical and the process was confined to damaging the church and removing the roofs and stairs of other buildings, leaving them open to the elements, uninhabitable and subject to dilapidation and decay. There would have been no need to preserve Newstead's church for parochial use when there was already a large, stone church less than a mile away in Uffington village and many more in Stamford. Henry Digby[1] at Belvoir Castle referred to the 'plucking down' of buildings at Newstead[2] (Foden, personal communication). Reduced to ruins, the site may have been leased as a quarry (Knowles [a] (vi)) or its stone and other building materials may simply have been scavenged for new buildings and roads. While it was a condition of sale that the church and conventual buildings should be razed to the ground, buildings beyond the church and cloister that might be of use to the new owner or farmer of the property would normally be spared (Knowles [a] (vi)).

Grants of the seized lands and property were soon made on long lease or by sales. Local landowners, who were often founders or patrons of a particular house, were among the principal purchasers of land in the first year or two (Knowles [a] (iii)). The Manners family of Belvoir were beneficiaries of this situation. At the Dissolution, Uffington manor was held by Thomas Manners (c.1492–1543), 12th Baron de Ros, who had been created 1st Earl of Rutland in 1525 (Sheehan [b] (i)) and was rebuilding Belvoir Castle. In 1538/39 Henry VIII granted the site and buildings of Newstead Priory to Thomas' younger brother, Richard Manners (LAO [c]), thereby returning it to a descendant of its founder (Fig.6).

Around the same time, Henry Digby, comptroller to the first earl, compiled four volumes of notes on all of the ex-monastic lands in the region (Foden, personal communication). Evidently many of the lands and properties which belonged to the late priory of Newstead by Stamford were acquired by the Earl of Rutland himself. A large grant of land and property was commonly accompanied by permission to alienate and acquisitions were often resold soon afterwards (Knowles [a] (iii)). In 1543 the earl sold to a consortium of Henry Digby, Robert Thurston, Roger Forest and John Netlam 'all his manors, messuages, etc.' in Braunston on the Hill in Northamptonshire, Ketton, Little Casterton and Tolethorpe in Rutland, and Grayingham, Colsterworth and Stamford in Lincolnshire, which had previously belonged to the Uffington priory (Rogers (iii)). The former priory lands in Little Casterton later passed to the Brownes, who probably acquired the Crown title from Richard Manners (Page [e]). This aggrieved John Fenton who complained to the Court of Augmentations that he had received a 50-year lease of the manor of Little Casterton from the late prior but that Francis Browne, disputing his claim, had enclosed lands in the manor and impounded his cattle (Page [e]). Because Richard Manners' only son, John, died without direct heirs, the priory site later passed into the hands of the 12th baron's descendants until 1673 when it was bought by Charles Bertie (Sheehan [b] (i)).

Fig.6 Gift and Grant letters patent under the Great Seal of Henry VIII, 13 March 1538/9 (Newstead by Stamford), granting the dissolved Newstead Priory to Richard Manners (Reproduced courtesy of Lincolnshire Archives Office: CRAGG 5/1/231)

Footnotes

1. Alternatively, Harry Dygby

2. Misc MS 107 folio 62

13. Analysis of the Priory Site

Few observations can be made about the largely-unexplored ground on the north side of the A1175 road. However, a walkover survey of land between Newstead Mill and the main road in 2013 found no visible traces of archaeological remains in the guise of either artefacts or earthworks. Prior to becoming a large garden associated with the adjacent former tollbar house, the site was predominantly agricultural, perhaps pasture (Cope-Faulkner), and possibly was part of the priory demesne. The two fields in that position in the mid-nineteenth century were jointly known as Flash Meadow, implying that the land was waterlogged or swampy (Cope-Faulkner). A trial trench evaluation undertaken for the Environment Agency in 2015 of an area of meadow bounded by the Gwash and the mill lade, and less than a quarter of a mile due west of Newstead Mill, likewise revealed no archaeological features (Sutherland and Trott).

As noted in Section 4, the topography of the Newstead end of Uffington Park is uneven and undulating.

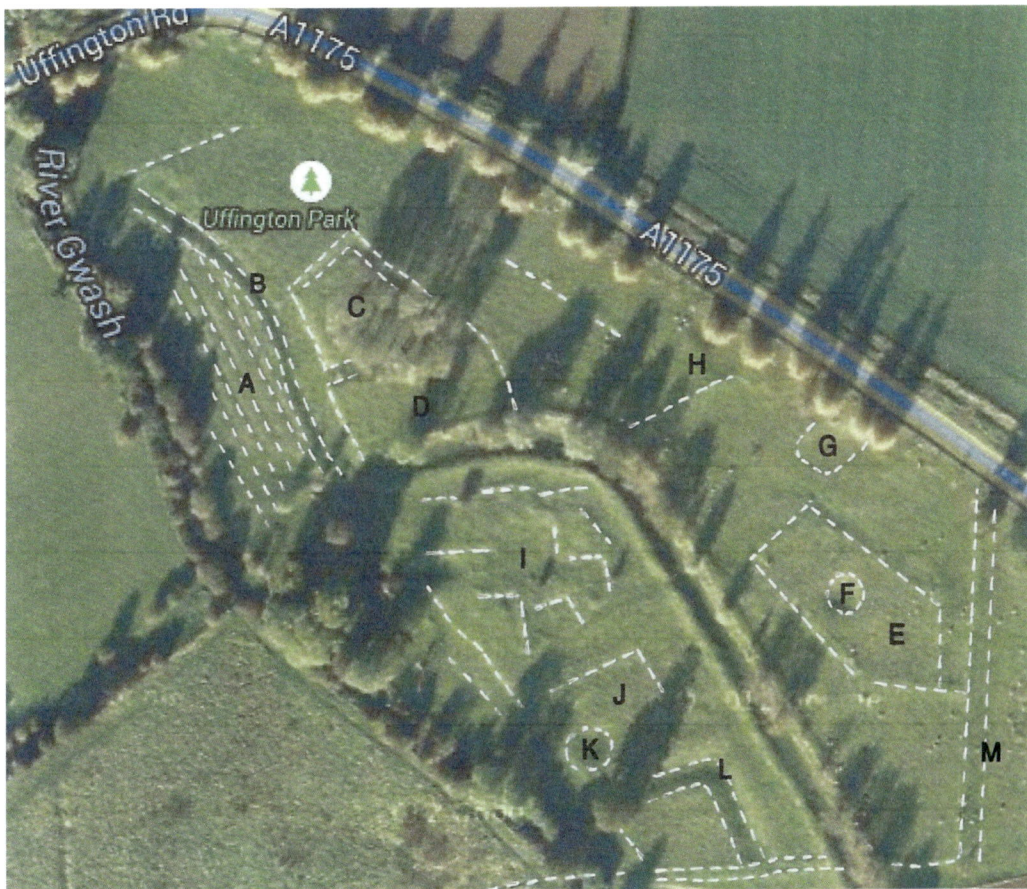

Fig.7 Detail of Fig.4 with the ground markings delineated (© 2018 Google/ Image © 2018 Getmapping plc)

On the north-west side is a sharply-defined area of a ridge and furrow field system (Murray and Cope-Faulkner) [A] (Fig.7)[1], encompassed by the River Gwash and a ditch [B]. The ditch represents a former twin channel of the river, as depicted in early-nineteenth-century maps (Fig.8). Both channels communicated with the canal, creating a central island.

Fig.8 Map extract from a survey of the Earl of Lindsey's Uffington estate in 1820

The ridge and furrow of this island and the adjacent smaller island [C] were identified as osier beds in a survey of the Earl of Lindsey's lands and properties in Uffington in 1820 (Bunham and Arden). They correspond to the osier beds referred to in local press reports, at the turn of the twentieth century, of otter hunts on the River Gwash, near the bridge (*Mercury* [b]). The present ditches surrounding [C] tally with its earlier water-filled boundaries (Fig.8). Below [C] a discrete rectangular area [D] abuts on the bank of the canal.

While some of the earthworks in this area of Uffington Park may be the result of the engineering works which enabled the canal to intersect with the River Gwash, several others offer compelling evidence to be the foundations of buildings. Immediately south-west of the Horse shoe Hurn gate, linear ridges come together to form an irregular pentagon [E] (Fig.7), compatible with the footprint of a substantial edifice. At its centre is a crater of approximately ten feet in depth [F]. Between this distinctive formation and the main road is a small depressed square with proud edges [G], also about ten feet at its deepest and tapering away from the road. North-west of this is another depression with a well-defined ridge crossing its base [H].

On the opposite side of the canal, certain faint surface outlines are suggestive of other built structures. The rough-textured area [I] in the crook of the canal, assumed at first sight to represent upcast from the excavation of the navigation, appears to overlie a number of squared outlines which may be compatible with structural foundations. Immediately south of [I] is an earthwork [J] (partly obscured by shadow on the satellite image) with a raised squared edge; at its bottom left-hand corner is a circular hollow [K], some three to six feet deep. Below it, a large, broad, inverted L-shaped ditch, or moat, [L] fills with water when the Gwash bursts its banks (Fig.9). The linear hollow way [M] is likely to be the track which was excavated for the carriage drive in the mid-nineteenth century.

Fig.9 View westwards along the flooded public footpath on the southern boundary of the priory site (March 2016). Flood water fills the northern (solid arrow) and eastern (open arrow) channels of the 'moat'

If [A] was part of a larger field system extending to the west, the rest will have been obliterated by the work carried out to level the terrain for the present sports ground (Cope-Faulkner). The same would be true for the remains of any priory buildings erected to the west of the Gwash. Any built structures or agricultural features to the south of the site would also have been obliterated when those fields were deep ploughed.

Significantly, the report for the proposed golf course commented that many of the numerous earthworks observed during field-walking of the site were visible only with difficulty from the air (Hall and Ford). It can be inferred that the satellite image also underestimates the extent of the earthworks. It is also the case that some of the ridges shown on the satellite image are less regular and definite when observed at ground level. Alternative explanations proffered for some of the earthworks include gravel quarries worked for construction of the road, and Second World War bomb craters (Hall and Ford).[2] Inevitably, some of the mounds and hollows will transpire to be natural formations.

Although scanty, other archaeological discoveries support the former presence of a medieval community in the area. A trench dug towards the west end of the site during the golf course survey yielded a body-sherd from a partially-glazed, decorated, tripod pitcher dated to the thirteenth or fourteenth century, contemporary with the priory. The small, crude head of a female statue, cast from lead or a heavy lead alloy, was found a short distance beyond the eastern extremity of the site. Deemed to be of medieval date, perhaps fourteenth century, it was discovered along with copper-alloy sheet fragments, also almost certainly medieval, which may have been from a book mount (Hall and Ford). These could have belonged to the priory.

The earthworks and artefacts challenge the view that the priory was 'small and insignificant' (Page [a]), or at least that this was always so. Unfortunately, the earthworks are insufficiently distinct to allow a ground plan to be formulated for even part of the site. Moreover, without standing walls or fallen or displaced architectural elements, no conclusions can be drawn about the superstructures of the lost buildings. With the passage of time, various buildings would have been enlarged, reconstructed or replaced to reflect changing circumstances and needs and perhaps even architectural fashion. Thus, the fragmentary earthworks may represent a mixture of buildings that came and went over a period of 300 years.

While it was customary for monasteries to be erected alongside a river (or other source of fresh water), it is improbable that de Albini would have built his hospital on land which was prone to flooding. The flood map published by the Environment Agency (Fig.10) shows the areas around Newstead which are most susceptible to flooding by the rivers Gwash and Welland. The threat was greater before the construction of Rutland Water reservoir, which was completed by the Water Board in the mid-1970s. Set on a gently sloping section of the north side of the Welland valley, most of the priory buildings would have been above the floodplain. However, whereas the parkland to the north of the canal tends to remain dry, the lower area between the canal and the Gwash is liable to flood following heavy rain. Whilst the heaviest inundation occurs beyond the public footpath running along its southern border, flooding can also occur within the boundaries of the site (Fig.9).

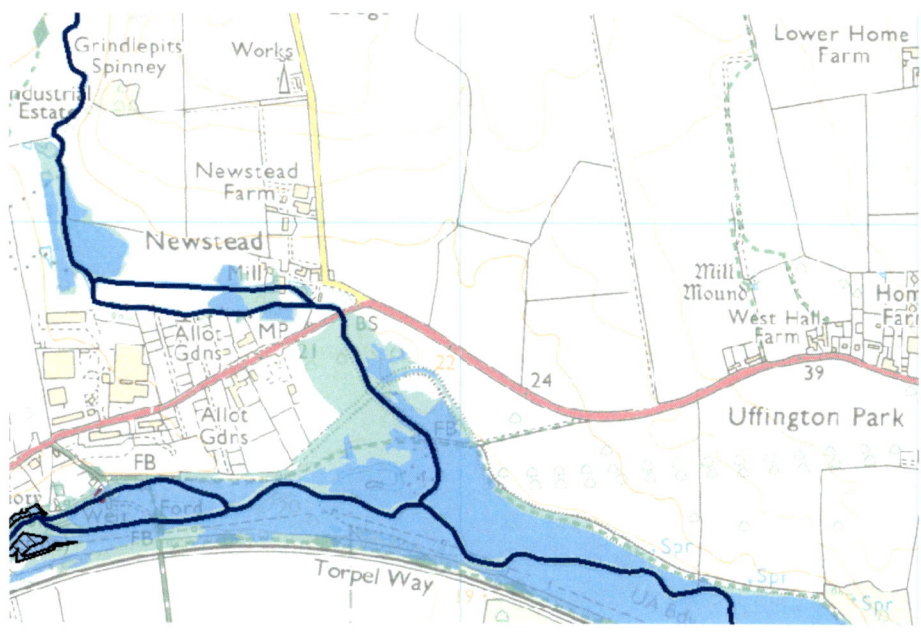

Fig.10 Environment Agency Flood Map for the Newstead area (Ordnance Survey Crown copyright). The darker blue shading shows the area most at risk of flooding from the rivers Gwash and Welland

If the monastery precinct extended northwards from the park, this could reconcile the otherwise-contradictory interpretations of the priory's location. If it did indeed stretch from the vicinity of Newstead Mill in the north to the southernmost earthworks in the park, a distance of almost a third of a mile, this would imply that Newstead by Stamford Priory was much larger than has hitherto been assumed. Most of the northerly part of the site would have been disturbed and obliterated by the re-routing of the Stamford–Deepings turnpike road in the 1830s.

Once satisfied that the west end of Uffington Park is the true location of at least part of the lost priory, the next major challenge is to interpret the ground markings in terms of individual buildings.

Footnotes

1. Another area of ridge and furrow to the east of the site (Cope-Faulkner) is less obvious.

2. The depressions and hollows on the south side of the Gwash are deemed to be the in-filled meanders of former courses of the Welland (Cope-Faulkner) but might equally be those of the Gwash itself.

14. Composition of the Priory

It is impossible to infer anything with certainty about the scale, composition or configuration of Newstead by Stamford Priory from the indeterminate physical remains within Uffington Park. This is because almost nothing is known about the number, variety and layout of its constituent buildings, given that there is no written description let alone any surviving maps, plans, other drawings or even an artist's impression. Furthermore, regardless of whether they are interpreted favourably as monastic remains, the visible earthworks could account for only a fraction of the minimum complement of buildings required by a small autonomous priory.

Little can be deduced about the architectural style and physical layout of the priory from the meagre clues in the corner of the park. Houses of Augustinian canons varied considerably in size and nature (Dickinson [b]). Valuations of Newstead Priory may give some indication of its size but the number and distribution of its buildings can only be guessed. Notwithstanding this, it would be natural for its master masons and builders to have taken their inspiration from other monasteries.

The pre-existing buildings that we know of from the early charters are the bridge chapel, the adjacent 'house' and the Uffington mill (Peck (ii)). Typically, the bridge chapel would have been built either into the bridge structure or immediately adjacent to the bridge. The earliest bridge chapels were constructed in the twelfth century and it was not unusual for them to be dedicated to Our Lady, or The Blessed Virgin Mary.

Whereas Peck interpreted 'tota curia adjacente' in William de Albini III's first charter (Dugdale) as 'the whole house adjacent' to the chapel (Peck (ii)), a valid alternative translation of 'curia' is 'court' (Drakard), which would imply a wider range of buildings. Although these were not specified, they would presumably be related to the workings of the mill, such as a mill office, granary, workshops, storage sheds, cart shed and stables, and they would probably have retained their original functions when subsumed into the priory. Explicit references have also been made to a church, a chapterhouse and an infirmary. In 1427 the Papal Register spoke of the church and priory buildings being 'ruinous with age' (Willis, F E d'A), while Bishop Alnwick's visit in 1440 took place in the chapterhouse (Thompson [b]). The original seven residents stayed in the infirmary (LAO [b]). Evidence for other core buildings is indirect. Observance of the Rule of Augustine demanded a common refectory and dormitory (Dickinson [a] (viii)) and these would have necessitated a kitchen and sanitary facilities. William de Albini IV described the priory as being enclosed with a wall and a ditch (Peck (iii)) and it can be inferred that access was via a gatehouse (Bramley). Thus there is both explicit and implicit evidence of several of the fundamental components of a medieval monastery at Newstead. Still others can be assumed.

It has been surmised that Newstead's bridge chapel of St Mary was adapted for the purposes of the house (Franklin M J). It must have initially served as a temporary church since William de Albini III stated that the master and assistant canon should celebrate daily [mass] in the chapel 'for the quick and the dead' (Peck (ii)). Subsequently, a new and larger house of worship will have been erected. This will have been completed at least by the time that the hospital was upgraded to a priory, given that William de Albini IV spoke of the 'church of the blessed Mary of Newstede' (Peck (iii)). However, nothing definite is known about the church. Although the Augustinians had a penchant in the early-twelfth century for aisleless churches built to a cruciform plan, the popularity of this style was waning by the thirteenth century (Franklin JA). If an aisle was added to a rudimentary church building at a later stage in the development and growth of the monastery, it might have been confined to the opposite side of the nave from the cloister (Hodgson), a second passageway on the other side being precluded by the presence of the claustral buildings. The discovery of fragments of an ambulatory in the nineteenth century (*Linc Chron*) suggests that the church had at least one aisle. The church would have been the largest building of the priory (Coppack).

Unless Newstead's church and domestic accommodation were basic and laid out in an L-shaped plan (Dickinson [b]), they would have been arranged around the four sides of a cloister, the individual ranges being connected by covered cloister alleys. While there was considerable variety in the ground plans of Augustinian monasteries (Heale), and there was no special monastic style, the cloister was usually on the south side of the church in northern climates to protect those living and working there from the cold north winds (Bramley; Gasquet). This was where the canons contemplated, studied, exercised, washed before meals and even did their laundry (Coppack). Under the traditional scheme, the sacristy, chapter house and dormitory would have been on the east side of the cloister, the refectory and kitchen on the south and the cellarer's range on the west with the prior's accommodation above it. If it did not occupy its own self-contained building, one or more rooms in the cloister ranges may have served as the infirmary (Coppack). The main latrine would have been positioned somewhere between the dormitory and the refectory and there would have been a lavatorium (washing place) at the entrance to the refectory (Burton, Janet). A room may not have been set aside specifically for a library, with books and manuscripts being kept instead in cupboards in the church, cloister or other buildings (Gasquet). The extent of Newstead's library is unknown. Sadly, when Henry VIII's antiquary, John Leland, toured Lincolnshire taking a record of the manuscripts held in its monasteries, he did not visit any house to the south of Boston or west of Lincoln (Liddell).

Assuming that Newstead conformed to the commonly-adopted pattern, its subsidiary buildings would have been arranged in an inner and an outer court beyond the domestic ranges of the cloister. The inner court normally housed the guest accommodation and stables, servants' quarters, bake house, brew house, laundry, the granaries providing for the day-to-day needs of the house, a kiln house for drying the grain for storage, and storerooms (Burton, Janet; Coppack). The outer court would have contained the agricultural and industrial buildings including, as appropriate, the great barns and granaries, craftsmen's workshops, smithy, cart house, animal houses and pens (Coppack), dovecotes, orchards, gardens (Burton, Janet), and stock ponds for fresh-water fish such as carp and trout sourced from the Gwash. According to custom (Coppack), Newstead's mill would also have been situated in the outer court. The distribution of buildings would have been dependent upon space constraints within the priory precinct. The granaries and major barns used for storing grain and other dry goods from the monastery's estates, and animal houses such as stables, byres and pigsties, might have been consigned to a nearby grange (Coppack). A lease granted in 1529 by the prior and convent of Newstead to Robert Haver of Stamford, of a close called 'northmylne hollme'[1] and a parcel of meadow called 'ye Kychyn meydow' (kitchen meadow) on the west side of their house (Rogers (v)), indicates that the priory lands, including the kitchen garden, extended to the north and west of the priory.

Burial in a monastery was highly coveted in medieval England because it ensured that the soul of the deceased would be prayed for regularly by the religious community (Heale). The church was the traditional burial place of the founder and his family (Coppack). While the walkways of the cloister and cloister garth were the customary places of burial for the community, cemeteries could also be located in other parts of the grounds, particularly to the north or around the east end of the monastery church (Coppack). William de Albini III and his wife Agatha were buried at Newstead by Stamford (Westerhof; Eller (i)), probably in the choir of the church as was conventional for the founder in the thirteenth century (Coppack). Following the popular practice of the time (Drury), William's heart was sent to Belvoir and buried to the north side of the high altar. A plaque bearing the inscription, '*Hic jacet cor Dni Willielmi Albiniaci, cujus corpus sepelitur apud novum locum juxta Stamfordiam*'[2], attesting to these burial arrangements, was removed to Bottesford Church at the Dissolution but later lost (Eller (i)). Leland was misinformed when he said that William II and William IV de Albini were also buried at Newstead Priory (Smith, LT). Both were interred in Belvoir Priory church (Eller (ii)) with their wives (Page [d]), while William IV's heart was buried at Croxton Kerrial Abbey in Leicestershire (Westerhof; Peck (viii)). It is equivocal whether just the heart, or both the heart and body, of Lady Isabella de Ros was buried at Newstead in 1301 (Peck (xi)). Leland's erroneous information about her father and great grandfather may actually have pertained to later descendants since the bodies of several members of the de Ros family were at first interred at Newstead (Willis, F E d'A) before being transferred in their leaden coffins (Eller (iii)) to Bottesford Church after the Dissolution (Peck (xi)). Not every de Ros who died at Uffington was buried at Newstead, one exception being Thomas de Ros (d.1383), brother and heir to William de Ros III, who was buried at Rievaulx Abbey (Eller (iv)). No human remains have been found at Newstead, suggesting that the priory did not offer burial space for the wider lay community, but it would be surprising if the canons themselves were not laid to rest there.

Newstead by Stamford's early temporary or subsidiary buildings may have been constructed in timber, with many of them being replaced later by others built in stone and roofed with slate or tile. Commonly, the church was the first masonry building to be constructed (Burton, Janet). Wherever possible, monastic builders used local material resources for their projects (Burton, Janet). Newstead's masons would have been particularly well served in this regard, the nearest quarry being less than three miles away at Barnack, whose durable freestone was used for Peterborough and Ely cathedrals. Timber sourced from the neighbouring woodlands would have been in constant demand not only for building but also, along with turf, as a fuel to heat the rooms of the house, for baking and brewing, and to feed the fires of the hearths in the kitchen (Coppack). If brick was another material used in construction, the manufacture of bricks and tiles in-house would very likely have availed of the local Jurassic clays, including Uffington's own, which centuries later would entice John Marriott Blashfield to move his renowned terracotta works from London to a new location in Stamford, just one mile from Newstead (Sheehan [b] (iii)). A forge would have been a basic requirement for the priory in view of the vast amounts of iron needed for the construction and repair of buildings, shoeing of horses and oxen, and the manufacture and maintenance of agricultural equipment (Coppack). The walls of the church and principal domestic buildings may have been plastered, painted with limewash, and lightly decorated; windows may have been glazed and floors tiled (Coppack). Water would have been conveyed by lead pipes (Coppack).[3] To what extent these generalisations apply to Newstead by Stamford is a matter of conjecture.

Although Prior Lylleforde complained in 1440 that the house had been almost ruined by the alienations of property made by his immediate predecessor (Thompson [b]), it is clear that what remained was very considerable. Along with the other local monasteries, Newstead appears to have escaped the fate of several of Stamford's medieval churches, which were reputedly damaged and burnt in 1461 when the town was sacked by Lancastrian forces during the Wars of the Roses. Henry VIII's gift and grant to Richard Manners in 1538/9, when distributing the spoils of the Dissolution, included the whole house and site of the late Newstead Priory, along with its church, bell tower and cemetery, and all messuages, houses, buildings, granges, gardens, dovecotes, orchards and lands both within and outside the site. Also included was the prior's manor overlapping the borders of Lincolnshire, Northamptonshire, Leicestershire and Rutland, 281 acres of arable land, 28 acres of meadow and 8 acres of pasture in Uffington, which formerly belonged to the monastery (Newstead), and all manors, messuages, granges, lands, etc. in Newstead by Stamford, Uffington, Casewick, Stamford, Little Casterton, Ketton, Braunston, Grayingham, Bottesford and Colsterworth (amongst other places), which were held by Newstead in the time of the last prior, John Blakett (LAO [c]).[4] This testifies to the prodigious extent of the priory's estate.

It is reasonable to assume that the priory demesne and the lands and properties in the immediate vicinity remained substantially intact for some time as they passed through the hands of successive owners. In 1673 Charles Bertie bought the site of Newstead Priory from the mortgagees of the 2nd Duke of Buckingham, together with the duke's former Uffington, Newstead and Tallington estates (Sheehan [b] (i)). Most of the Newstead land was subsequently acquired by the Bellairs-Stevenson family and in 1844 James Peel Stevenson (1808–1897) inherited the corn mill and other properties and lands on the north side of the turnpike road. When put up for lease in 1858 the Newstead property included the new steam and water corn mill, the mill house, cottages, barns, outbuildings and premises, along with several closes and parcels of land and cottages and outbuildings belonging to them, the whole amounting to just over 238 acres (*Lond Gaz*).

Footnotes

1. Interpreted as 'a piece of flat ground north of the mill which was subject to flooding'

2. 'Here lies the heart of William de Albini whose body was buried at Newstead near Stamford'

3. A riverside location was frequently chosen for a religious house because of the huge quantities of water required for drinking, cooking, washing, flushing drains, filling fish ponds and servicing the buildings of the outer court.

4. The list is incomplete because some of the place names are difficult to decipher and identify in the original document granting Newstead to Richard Manners.

15. Physical Remains, Relics and Effigies

As already described, the known physical remains of the priory are confined to earthworks at the west end of Uffington Park, and hitherto no traces have been found of monastic buildings close to Newstead Mill. There is no indication as to whether the original bridge chapel was located on the north or the south side of the medieval bridge, which might have provided a clue to the subsequent direction of development of the priory precinct. By 1727 Newstead's surrounding wall had been knocked down and the ditch filled in (Peck (iii)). Peck surmised that a section of the ditch might have been incorporated into the canal when it was cut across the site in the seventeenth century. An implication of this would be that the canal channel defines part of the boundary of the priory. However, it is more likely that the southern boundary was delineated by the course of the Gwash as it approached its confluence with the Welland, taking into account that a monastery precinct was sometimes bounded by a stream as well as by the outer wall (Bramley).

Regardless of how its buildings met their fate, by the early-eighteenth century there were no remains of either the church or priory other than some traces of the foundations and other building remnants just above the ground (Peck (iii)). The surviving foundations have probably remained undisturbed since the completion of Stamford Canal.

It has been said that the external wall of the Trollope (Casewick) chapel at Uffington Church (Fig.11) originally formed part of St Mary's Priory and chapel at Newstead (*Mercury* [c]). Casewick Chapel was erected in the late-fifteenth century but a pointed arch and an incomplete round arch in its west wall show that there was an earlier building in that position (Sheehan [b] (iv)). If the present outer wall of the Trollope chapel were to have come from Newstead, this would imply that the priory's chapel was one of the later buildings of the monastery. Moreover, the wall would be the only substantial structure to have survived the destruction inflicted on the house after the Dissolution. While this notion is unsubstantiated and dubious, the architectural style of Casewick Chapel may nonetheless reflect the appearance of Newstead's ecclesiastical buildings in the latter years of the priory.

Fig.11 Casewick (Trollope) Chapel (2017)

Very few objects associated with the priory remain. One important exception is an impression on red wax of the common seal of Newstead by Stamford attached to the Acknowledgement of Supremacy, which shows seated figures of a man and a woman within an incomplete legend (Fig.12) (Dugdale). Originally held in the Chapter House at Westminster, it is now in The National Archives at Kew (E25/91). The legend is damaged and indecipherable but previously the remnant read: 'SIGILLV. COE...ORAT.NOVI.LOCI.......'.

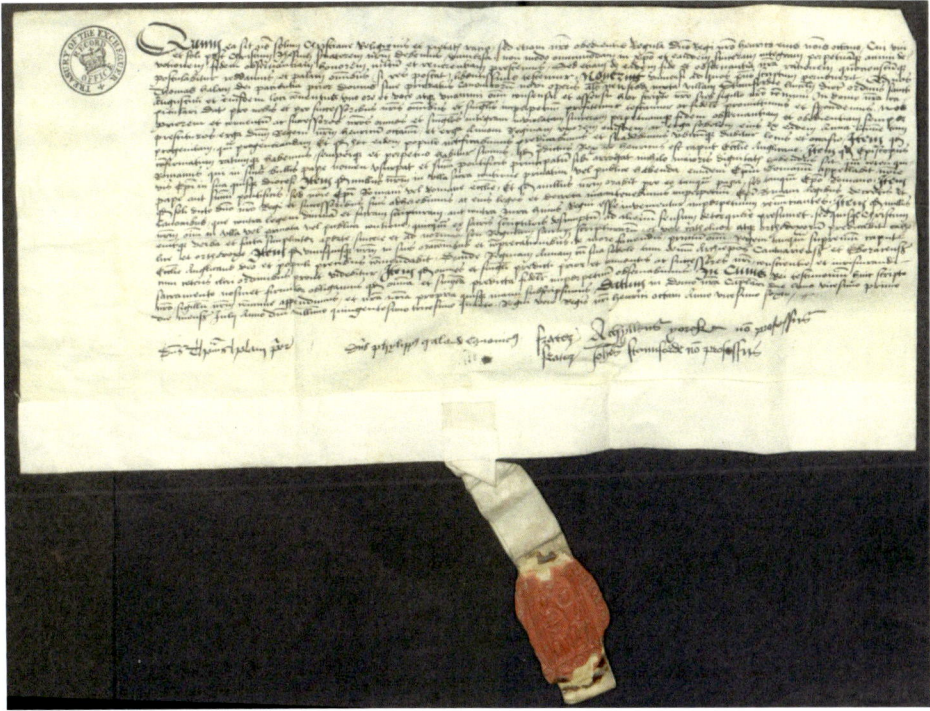

Fig.12 Acknowledgement of Supremacy for Newstead by Stamford (Image supplied by The National Archives: E25/91–Newstead by Stamford, Lincs; prior and convent of the Priory. Date 21 July 1534)

Artefacts have come to light sporadically. Notable finds in 1863 included a portion of a statue of a warrior at the time of Henry III, an ancient freestone probably from an ambulatory, some thirteenth-century jamb shafts, and a great quantity of window tracery of the fourteenth century (*Linc Chron*). Some of these specimens were collected up and retained and others were expected to be revealed as the excavation of the carriageway proceeded. The hand of the statue found amongst the debris was to be preserved at Uffington House (Mercury [a]). Regrettably, these relics, like the buildings themselves before them, have disappeared without trace and there is no indication that an inventory was taken. There is no record of whether any vestiges of the priory were uncovered when the Stamford–Deepings turnpike road was diverted in the 1830s, but trenches dug on a short stretch of Newstead Lane at Newstead corner in 2018, for maintenance work on the water mains, revealed no recognisable artefacts (personal observation). No spreads of rubble, slates, tiles, pottery or glass have been reported in the ploughed soil of arable fields surrounding the priory site.

A seal attached to the charter granting the church of Redmile to the church of St Mary at Belvoir bears a representation of William de Albini III on horseback (Fig.13) (Carrington). Other charters preserved at Belvoir Castle also carry his seal.

Fig.13 Seal on Redmile Charter 90 in Belvoir Castle muniments room (By permission of His Grace the Duke of Rutland)

No other confirmed image of William de Albini III is known to exist. Affixed to the north wall of the chancel in Bottesford Church, a small figure of Purbeck marble, about 21 in. high and depicting a late-thirteenth-century knight (Fig.14), was traditionally determined to be a monumental sculpture of Robert de Todeni. This attribution was challenged in the mid-nineteenth century when it was posited that it was a commemorative emblem of William de Albini III (Eller (v)) or, more specifically, his heart effigy or shrine (*Mercury* [d]; Drury). However, the figure is now deemed to be that of Robert de Ros (d.1285), husband of William III's granddaughter Isabel, since it was originally at Croxton Abbey where Robert's heart was buried (Medieval Combat Society).

A stone effigy of a recumbent knight in St Michael and All Angels Church at Uffington was also thought to be that of Willliam de Albini III, in the belief that it had been removed from Newstead Priory to the parish church at the Dissolution. It was ultimately identified from its armour and

Fig.14 Effigy in Bottesford Church

46

heraldry as that of Richard de Schropshire (d.c.1418), Constable of Belvoir, who bought Casewick Hall in 1392 (Sheehan [b] (v)). The newspaper correspondent who believed that the external wall of Casewick Chapel had originated at Newstead Priory may have been influenced by the story surrounding this reposing figure built into the inner wall of the chapel.

If there are no certain representations of William de Albini III, there is one of his granddaughter, Isabel de Ros. The early-fourteenth-century, six-foot long, stone, female effigy in the Church of St Mary at Orston in Nottinghamshire (Fig.15) is plausibly deemed to have come from Newstead Priory church (Gill). There is no inscription but traces of lineage are borne on two small shields above the shoulders, one for de Ros, Lords of Belvoir, and the other consistent with the coat of arms of the de Albinis of Belvoir and Uffington. The combination of the arms of de Albini and de Ros and the early-fourteenth-century date point to the effigy being that of Isabel.

(a)

(b)

Fig.15 (a) Effigy of Isabel de Ros; (b) Detail of head of monument

In 2013 a resident of Newstead hamlet dug up a stone crocket (Fig.16) from the front garden of his cottage on the approach to the mill. This may have been part of a Corinthian capital or have adorned a pinnacle on (or in) the priory church. The location of the find cannot be taken to indicate the site of the monastery, whose stones were no doubt dispersed far and wide after the Dissolution.

(a)   (b)

Fig.16 Crocket: (a) obverse; (b) profile

Other architectural stones have also been found at Newstead but it is uncertain whether they came from the priory. The most compelling is one (Fig.17) which may have supported a wooden post or pillar in the monastery.[1]

Fig.17 Possible plinth for a wooden pillar

Apart from these scanty examples, no relics of the priory or its estate have been unearthed in recent memory within a quarter of a mile radius to the north, east or west of Newstead Mill, although some have been discovered further afield. Numerous fragments of Early-English masonry were dug up in a close westward of Little Casterton Church in the early 1860s (*Mercury* [e])[2] and the extensive structure disclosed by the uneven surface of the ground was suspected of having been the prior's mansion.

A disappointingly small number of documents relating to Newstead by Stamford have been identified in private collections. In one of his commonplace books, Henry Digby referred to a survey book of Newstead (Foden, personal communication) but this does not appear to be amongst the muniments at Belvoir Castle. It is intriguing to speculate that it might be the 'curious book' which Peck assumed had been lost at the Suppression. William Stukeley wrote in his Diary for September 1745: 'The Rev. Mr. Bertie of Uffington, visited me. His brother has many old records relating to Newstead priory.' (Stukeley). Thus far, no such records or any note-worthy documents or objects relating to the priory have surfaced in the archive of the Uffington Berties, which is held in a private collection in the Scottish Borders; however, most of the collection is in storage and currently inaccessible. Unfortunately, cartularies attributed to Newstead Priory in various archives (Davis, G R C) have more often belonged to Newstead Abbey than to the Uffington house.

Footnotes

1. A more prosaic suggestion (based on the interpretation of photographs rather than the physical item) is that it might have been a chicken or duck feeder (Stocker, personal communication).
   Object photographed by kind permission of Lorraine and Jerry Thurston.

2. These included deeply-moulded arch pieces, clustered jamb or window shafts, hood mould terminations consisting of heads etc.

16. Conclusion

Newstead by Stamford appears to have been a larger and more important priory than it has hitherto been given credit for. Between its humble beginnings and its ignominious end, it reached its apotheosis in the fourteenth century when its complement of canons peaked at seven and it hosted at least six general chapters of the Augustinian order. It will require a detailed archaeological survey with techniques such as aerial photography and 3D laser scanning, geophysical technologies, and excavation to obtain confirmation of the priory's location and give an indication of the nature and extent of its buildings. In 2015 the Uffington Conservation Area boundary was extended to include Uffington Park (South Kesteven District Council), a measure which should safeguard the site of the priory for future evaluation. Such a study would give an invaluable insight into the lives of the Augustinian Canons in South Lincolnshire.

References

Bunham, J and Arden, E. Uffington Valuation, 1820. *Surveys of the Estates of the Earl of Lindsey* (Original copy held at Uffington)

Burton, Geo. *Chronology of Stamford* (Stamford: Bagley, 1846), pp.231–32

Caley, John, Ellis, Henry and Bandinel, Bulkeley. Priory of Belvoir, in Lincolnshire: A Cell to the Abbey of St. Albans. *Monasticon Anglicanum.* Vol. 3. New edition (Originally published by Sir William Dugdale) (London, 1846), pp.284–93

Cameron, Kenneth. *A Dictionary of Lincolnshire Place-Names.* English Place-Name Society Popular Series, Vol. 1 (Nottingham: English Place-Name Society, 1998), p.91

Carrington, W A. The Early Lords of Belvoir. *Journal of the British Archaeological Association.* New Series, Vol. VII (London, 1901), pp.299–326

Clubley, Clifford. *John de Dalderby, Bishop of Lincoln, 1300–1320.* PhD Thesis (Appendix A), University of Hull, 1965 <http://hydra.hull.ac.uk/assets/hull:6739a/content>

Cope-Faulkner, Paul. *Archaeological Desk-Based Assessment of Land at Uffington Road, Newstead, Stamford, Lincolnshire.* Archaeological Project Services Report No. 145/13 (December 2013)

Davis, F N (ed) [a]. *Rotuli Hugonis de Welles, Episcopi Lincolniensis, 1209–1235,* Vol. III (LRS 9) (Lincoln: Lincoln Record Society, 1914)

Davis, F N (ed.) [b]. *The Rolls of Robert Grosseteste and Henry Lexington, Bishops of Lincoln, 1235–1259* (LRS 11) (Horncastle: Lincoln Record Society, 1914), p.88

Davis, G R C. *Medieval Cartularies of Great Britain and Ireland.* Revised by Breay C, Harrison J and Smith D M (London, 2010), pp.140, 275–76, 282

Dickinson, J C [a]. *The Origins of the Austin Canons and their Introduction into England* (London: SPCK, 1950), pp.(i) 296; (ii) 146–47; (iii) 59; (iv) 185; (v) 193; (vi) 183; (vii) 142; (viii) 168

Dickinson, J C [b]. The Buildings of the English Austin Canons after the Dissolution of the Monasteries. *Journal of the British Archaeological Association,* Vol. 31 (London: British Archaeological Association, 1968), pp.60–75

Drakard, John. *The History of Stamford in the County of Lincoln* (Stamford: Drakard, 1822), pp.181–84

Drury, G Dru. Heart Burials and Some Purbeck Marble Heart-Shrines. *Proceedings of the Dorset Natural History and Antiquarian Field Club*, Vol. 48 (Dorchester: The Club, 1927), pp.38–58

Dugdale, William. Newstede Priory, in Lincolnshire. *Monasticon Anglicanum: A History of the Abbies and other Monasteries, Hospitals, Frieries, and Cathedral and Collegiate Churches, with their Dependencies, in England and Wales,* Vol. 6, Part 1 (London: Longman, Hurst, Rees, Orme and Brown, 1817–1830), pp.562–64

Eller, Rev Irvin. *The History of Belvoir Castle from the Norman Conquest to the Nineteenth Century* (London: Tyas and Groombridge, 1841), pp.(i) 12; (ii) 191; (iii) 348; (iv) 13; (v) 364

Eshelby, H D. Robert Exelby, Prior of Newstead and of Fineshed. *East Anglian*, New Series, 2 (1887–88), pp.127–28

Feudal Aids. Lincoln. *Inquisitions and assessments relating to Feudal Aids; with other analogous documents A.D. 1284–1431*, Vol. III (London: HMSO, 1904), pp.(i) 166; (ii) 210

Fletcher, Anthony and MacCulloch, Diarmaid. *Tudor Rebellions.* Sixth edition (Oxon: Routledge, 2016), p.23

Foster, C W (ed.). The Testament of Edward Watson of Liddington, co. Rutland. *Lincoln Wills*, Vol. III (A.D. 1530–1532) (London: Lincoln Record Society, 1930), pp.20–24

Franklin, Jill A. Augustinian Architecture in the Twelfth Century: The Context for Carlisle Cathedral. In: Carlisle and Cumbria: Roman and Medieval Architecture, Art and Archaeology. McCarthy, M and Weston, D (eds). *British Archaeological Association Conference Transactions*, Vol. 27 (Leeds: Maney, 2004), pp.73–88

Franklin, M J. The Beginnings of Newstead-by-Stamford Priory. *Lincolnshire History and Archaeology*, Vol.21 (Lincoln: Society for Lincolnshire History and Archaeology, 1986), pp.35–37

Frost, Judith A. Thornton Abbey: Canons and their Careers within the Cloister. In: Janet Burton and Karen Stober (eds). *The Regular Canons in the Medieval British Isles* (Turnhout: Brepols Publishers, 2011), pp.251–66

Gill, Harry. The Church of St. Mary, Orston. *Transactions of the Thoroton Society*, Vol. 24 (1920) <http://nottshistory.org.uk/articles/tts/tts1920/orston2.htm>

Greenway, Diana E (ed.). Bishops. In: *Fasti Ecclesiae Anglicanae 1066-1300*, Vol. 3 (Lincoln) (Originally published by Institute of Historical Research, London, 1977), pp.1–5. In: *British History Online* <http://www.british-history.ac.uk/fasti-ecclesiae/1066-1300/vol3/pp1-5> [accessed 9 April 2018]

Hall, Melanie and Ford, Steve. *An archaeological evaluation in advance of the proposed golf course development for the Trustees of the late Lady Muriel Barclay-Harvey.* Thames Valley Archaeological Services unpublished report series: Report 91/16 (1991) <http://www.archaeologydataservice.ac.uk/>

Harrod, W. *The Antiquities and Present State of Stamford and St. Martin's*, Vol.1 (Stamford: Harrod, 1785), pp.63–65

Hartley, John S and Rogers, Alan. Newstead Priory by Stamford. *The Religious Foundations of Medieval Stamford. Stamford Survey Group Report 2* (University of Nottingham, 1974), p.71

Hill, Rosalind M T (ed.) [a]. *The Rolls and Register of Bishop Oliver Sutton 1280–1299*, Vol. I (LRS 39) (Hereford: Lincoln Record Society, 1948), pp.(i) 99; (ii)70–71; (iii) 169; (iv) 3-4; (v) 25, 48

Hill, Rosalind M T (ed.) [b]. *The Rolls and Register of Bishop Oliver Sutton 1280–1299*, Vol. II (LRS 43) (Hereford: Lincoln Record Society, 1950), pp.4, 120

Hill, Rosalind M T (ed.) [c]. *The Rolls and Register of Bishop Oliver Sutton 1280–1299*, Vol. VII (LRS 69) (Lincoln: Lincoln Record Society, 1975), pp.xii–xiii; A124–7

Hill, Rosalind M T (ed.) [d]. *The Rolls and Register of Bishop Oliver Sutton 1280–1299*, Vol. IV (LRS 52) (Hereford: Lincoln Record Society, 1958), pp.33–36

Hill, Rosalind M T (ed.) [e]. *The Rolls and Register of Bishop Oliver Sutton 1280–1299*, Vol. V (LRS 60) (Hereford: Lincoln Record Society, 1965), pp.(i) 130,188,194; (ii) 69–70

Hill, Rosalind M T (ed.) [f]. *The Rolls and Register of Bishop Oliver Sutton 1280–1299*, Vol. VI (LRS 64) (Lincoln: Lincoln Record Society, 1969), pp.(i) 188; (ii) 95, 189

Hill, Rosalind M T (ed.) [g]. *The Rolls and Register of Bishop Oliver Sutton 1280–1299*, Vol. III (LRS 48) (Hereford: Lincoln Record Society, 1954), pp.xxiv–xxv

Historic England. Newstead Priory, Lincolnshire. *PastScape* <http://www.pastscape.org.uk/hob.aspx?hob_id=347954&sort=4&search=all&criteria=Newstead&rational=q&recordsperpage=60>

Historical Manuscripts Commission. *The Manuscripts of His Grace the Duke of Rutland, KG. Preserved at Belvoir Castle,* Vol. IV (London: HMSO, 1905), pp.(i) 144; (ii) 145

Hodgson, J F. On the difference of plan alleged to exist between churches of Austin canons and those of monks; and the frequency with which such churches were parochial. *Archaeological Journal,* Vol. 41 (Royal Archaeological Institute, 1884), pp.374–414

Hoskin, Philippa M (ed.). *Robert Grosseteste as Bishop of Lincoln. The Episcopal Rolls, 1235–1253* (Woodbridge: Lincoln Record Society, 2015)

Howgrave, Francis. *An Essay of the Ancient and Present State of Stamford* (Stamford, 1726), pp.98–99

Jack, S M. Dissolution Dates for the Monasteries Dissolved under the Act of 1536. *Bulletin of the Institute of Historical Research,* Vol. 43 (1970), p.173

Knowles, David [a]. *The Religious Orders in England.* Vol. III: The Tudor Age (Cambridge: Cambridge University Press, 1959), pp.(i) 241–59; (ii) 304-19; (iii) 393–401; (iv) 402–17; (v) 286–87; (vi) 383–88

Knowles, David [b]. *The Religious Orders in England.* Vol. I (Cambridge: Cambridge University Press, 1948), pp.(i) 276; (ii) 30

Knowles, David and Hadcock, R Neville. The Augustinian Canons. *Medieval Religious Houses England and Wales,* Second edition (First published 1953) (London: Longman, 1971), pp.137–80

LAO [a]. Lincolnshire Archives Office, *LAO KESTEVEN AWARD/80* (Plan of the Lordship of Uffington. 1794 Enclosure Award for Uffington)

LAO [b]. Lincolnshire Archives Office, *LAO Register XXVI ff. 122v–123r* (Episcopal Register of Bishop John Longland)

LAO [c]. Lincolnshire Archives Office, *LAO CRAGG 5/1/231* (Gift and grant of late priory of Newstead by Stamford)

Liber Feodorum. [Novo Loco juxta Stanford] *Liber Feodorum (Testa de Nevill).* Part II: A.D. 1242–1293 (First published in 1923 on behalf of the Public Record Office. Reprinted by permission of the Controller of Her Britannic Majesty's Stationery Office, 1971), pp.(i) 941, 945; (ii) 1052, 1091

Liddell, J R. 'Leland's' Lists of Manuscripts in Lincolnshire Monasteries. *English Historical Review,* Vol. 54 (213) (January 1939), pp.88–95

Linc Chron. Newstead Priory and Hospital. *Lincolnshire Chronicle,* 18 December 1863, p.8, col.1

Lincolnshire County Council. *The Priory of Newstead by Stamford, Uffington.* Lincolnshire Historic Environment Record Monument Report No. 33538-MLI33538 <http://www.heritagegateway.org.uk/Gateway/Results_Single.aspx?uid=MLI33538> [accessed 7 April 2015]

Lond Gaz. [Notice relating to leasing of Newstead Mill] *London Gazette,* 16 February 1858, p.789, col.2

Magna Carta Barons Association. William d'Albini <http://www.magnacartabarons.info/index.php/the-barons/albini-william-d/>

Medieval Combat Society. Bottesford St Mary <http://www.themcs.org/churches/Bottesford>

Medieval Genealogy. The National Archives. *Feet of Fines: CP 25/1/132/51, number 44* (Lincolnshire) <http://www.medievalgenealogy.org.uk/fines/lincolnshire.shtml>

Mercury [a]. [Exact site of Newstead Priory discovered and identity of a statue in the church at Uffington] *Lincoln, Rutland and Stamford Mercury,* 18 December 1863, p.4, col.2

Mercury [b]. *Lincoln, Rutland, and Stamford Mercury,* 21 September 1900, p.4; 6 September 1901, p.4

Mercury [c]. The Recumbent Effigy and Heraldry at Uffington Church [letter]. *Lincoln, Rutland, and Stamford Mercury,* 18 May 1866, p.6, col.4

Mercury [d]. An Interesting Relic. *Lincoln, Rutland, and Stamford Mercury,* 5 August 1864, p.6, col.5

Mercury [e]. [Prior of Newstead's mansion at Little Casterton] *Lincoln, Rutland, and Stamford Mercury,* 2 May 1862, p.4, col.2

Murray, Liz and Cope-Faulkner, Paul. *Archaeological Desk-Based Assessment Along the Proposed Route of an Eastern Relief Road, Stamford, Lincolnshire.* Archaeological Project Services Report No: 66/12 (October 2012) <http://www.southkesteven.gov.uk/chttphandler.ashx?id=7849>

Nevinson, Charles. *History of Stamford* (Stamford: Henry Johnson, 1879), pp.31–32

Nichols, Nick. The Augustinian Canons and Their Parish Churches: A Key to Their Identity. In: Janet Burton and Karen Stober (eds). *The Regular Canons in the Medieval British Isles* (Turnhout: Brepols Publishers, 2011), pp.313–37

Orme, Nicholas. The Augustinian Canons and Education. In: Janet Burton and Karen Stober (eds). *The Regular Canons in the Medieval British Isles* (Turnhout: Brepols Publishers, 2011), pp.213–32

Page, William (ed.) [a]. Houses of Austin canons: The priory of Newstead by Stamford. *A History of the County of Lincoln*, Vol. 2 (London, 1906), pp.176–77 (Originally published by Victoria County History) In: *British History Online* <http://www.british-history.ac.uk/vch/lincs/vol2/pp176-177> [accessed 7 October 2012]

Page, William (ed.) [b]. Houses of Austin canons: The priory of Newstead. *A History of the County of Nottingham,* Vol. 2 (London, 1910), pp.112–17 (Originally published by Victoria County History) In: *British History Online* <http://www.british-history.ac.uk/vch/notts/vol2> [accessed 23 February 2016]

Page, William (ed.) [c]. Houses of the Gilbertine order: The priory of Newstead-on-Ancholme. *A History of the County of Lincoln*, Vol. 2 (London, 1906), pp.197–98

(Originally published by Victoria County History) In: *British History Online* <http://www.british-history.ac.uk/vch/lincs/vol2/pp197-198> [accessed 23 February 2016]

Page, William (ed.) [d]. Houses of Benedictine monks: The priory of Belvoir. *A History of the County of Lincoln,* Vol. 2 (London, 1906), pp.124–27 (Originally published by Victoria County History) In: *British History Online* <http://www.british-history.ac.uk/vch/lincs/vol2/pp124-127> [accessed 14 January 2018]

Page, William (ed.) [e]. Parishes: Little Casterton. *A History of the County of Rutland,* Vol. 2 (London, 1935), pp.236-42 (Originally published by Victoria County History) In: *British History Online* <http://www.british-history.ac.uk/vch/rutland/vol2/pp236-242> [accessed 14 January 2018]

Page, William (ed.) [f]. Braunston. *An Inventory of the Historical Monuments in the County of Northamptonshire, Vol. 3, Archaeological Sites in North-West Northamptonshire* (London, 1981), pp.21–25 (Originally published by Her Majesty's Stationery Office) In: *British History Online* <http://www.british-history.ac.uk/rchme/northants/vol3/pp21-25> [accessed 14 January 2018]

Peck, Francis. *Academia tertia Anglicana (or, The Antiquarian Annals of Stanford)* (London, 1727 [Republished in 1979 by EP Publishing Ltd]), pp.(i) VIII XVI; (ii) VIII XIV; (iii) VIII XX; (iv) X II; (v) X VI; (vi) X XIV; (vii) XIV I; (viii) F9; (ix) IX XVII; (x) IX VIII; (xi) IX XXIX

Robinson, David M [a]. *The Geography of Augustinian Settlement in Medieval England and Wales,* Part i. BAR British Series 80(i) (Oxford, 1980)

Robinson, David M [b]. *The Geography of Augustinian Settlement in Medieval England and Wales,* Part ii. BAR British Series 80(ii) (Oxford, 1980)

Roffe, David (ed.). *Stamford in the Thirteenth Century: two inquisitions from the reign of Edward I* (Stamford: Paul Watkins, 1994), (i) Roll A14, p.49; (ii) Roll A11, p.47; Roll B11, p.60

Rogers, Alan (ed.). *People and Property in Medieval Stamford* (Bury St Edmunds: Abramis Academic Publishing, 2012), (i) 668. 7/12/10, pp.292–93; (ii) 687. 1.4. Ebor. 18c, p.300; (iii) 581. E326/8836, p.260; (iv) 775.TH 8A/1/8, pp.357–58; (v) 589. E326/11216, p.264

Salter, H (ed.). *A Subsidy Collected in the Diocese of Lincoln in 1526. I: Lincolnshire* (Oxford: Blackwell, 1909), p.91

Salter, H E (ed.). *Chapters of the Augustinian Canons* (Oxford Historical Society, Vol. 74) (Oxford, 1922)

Savine, Alexander. English Monasteries on the Eve of the Dissolution. In: Vinogradoff, Paul (ed.). *Oxford Studies in Social and Legal History,* Vol. I (Oxford, 1909)

Sheehan, N J [a]. Magna Carta and the Uffington Connection. *East Midlands History and Heritage,* Issue 2 (December 2015), pp.20–21

Sheehan, N J [b]. *Uffington in the County of Lincolnshire* (Stamford, 2014), pp.(i) 38–41; (ii) 18–19; (iii) 120–21; (iv) 80; (v) 61, 86

Sheehan, N J [c]. *Stamford University: the stuttering dream* (Stamford, 2012), pp.(i) 15–27; (ii) 28

Simons, Rosemary. The National Archives, *Edward IV, 1483: CP40no883* (Documents from Medieval and Early Modern England: Lincs, image 157)

Smith, David M (ed.). *The Heads of Religious Houses: England and Wales, III, 1377–1540* (Cambridge: Cambridge University Press, 2008), pp.489–90

Smith, David M and London, Vera C M (eds). *The Heads of Religious Houses: England and Wales, II, 1216–1377* (Cambridge: Cambridge University Press, 2001), pp.432–33

Smith, Lucy Toulmin (ed.). *The Itinerary of John Leland in or about the years 1535–1543,* Vol. IV, Parts VII and VIII (London: George Bell and Sons, 1909), p.89

South Kesteven District Council. *Uffington Conservation Area Appraisal and Management Plan* (2015 Review), p.4

STH [a]. Stamford Town Hall Library, *T65* (12 Essays on Stamford and the Neighbourhood–manuscript by E Bentley Wood)

STH [b]. Stamford Town Hall Archives, *Box 192* (Report of Thos Pear, dated 2 August 1823, regarding the projected repair and improvement of Newstead Bridge)

STH [c]. Stamford Town Hall Archives, *Box 192* (Copy agreement between Sir John Trollope and William A Johnson, dated 18 January 1832, regarding the erection of a new bridge at Newstead)

Stukeley, William. *Diary.* Vol. vii, p.97, September 1745

Sutherland, Donald and Trott, Kevin. *Land off Uffington Road, Newstead, Stamford, Lincolnshire: An Archaeological Evaluation.* Pre-Consruct Archaeology Ltd Report No. R12280 (November 2015)

Tanner, Thomas. *Notitia Monastica (or, An Account of all the Abbies, Priories, and Houses of Friers, heretofore in England and Wales and also of all the Colleges and Hospitals founded before A.D. MDXL)* (London,1744), p.280

Taxatio. [Novo Loco ext' Staunford] *Taxatio Ecclesiastica Angliae et Walliae auctoritate P. Nicholai IV. circa A.D. 1291* (Printed by Command of His Majesty King

George III in pursuance of an address of The House of Commons of Great Britain, London, 1802), p.69

Thompson, A Hamilton (ed.) [a]. Newstead priory by Stamford: Certificate of inquiry concerning the resignation of William Suttone, prior, 1435–6. *Visitations of Religious Houses in the Diocese of Lincoln,* Vol. I: Injunctions and Other Documents from the Registers of Richard Flemyng and William Gray, Bishops of Lincoln A.D. 1420–1436 (LRS 7) (Horncastle: Lincoln Record Society, 1914), pp.92–94

Thompson, A Hamilton (ed.) [b]. *Visitations of Religious Houses in the Diocese of Lincoln,* Vol. III: Records of Visitations held by William Alnwick Bishop of Lincoln A.D. 1436–1449, Part ii (LRS 21) (Lincoln: Lincoln Record Society, 1929), pp.240–41

Thompson, A Hamilton (ed.) [c]. *Visitations in the Diocese of Lincoln 1517–1531,* Vol. III: Visitations of Religious Houses (concluded) by Bishops Atwater and Longland and by their Commissaries, 1517-1531 (LRS 37) (Hereford: Lincoln Record Society, 1947), p.29

Valor. [Newsted jux Stamford] *Valor Ecclesiasticus Temp. Henr. VIII. Auctoritate Regia Institutus,* Vol. IV (Printed by Command of His Majesty King George III in pursuance of an address of The House of Commons of Great Britain, 1821), pp.109–10

Vincent, Nicholas. Aubigné, William d' [William de Albini] (d.1236). In: Matthew, H C G and Harrison, Brian (eds). *Oxford Dictionary of National Biography* (Oxford: Oxford University Press, 2004) <http://doi.org/10.1093/ref:odnb/284>

Walcott, Mackenzie E C. Churches, Monasteries, and Medieval Buildings wholly Destroyed. *Memorials of Stamford: Past and Present.* Third edition (Stamford: J H Howard, 1902), p.16

Westerhof, Danielle Marianne. *Aristocratic Executions and Burials in England c.1150–c.1330: Cultures of Fragmentation.* PhD Thesis (Appendix 1), University of York, 2004 <http://etheses.whiterose.ac.uk/ 9861/1/421597.pdf>

Willis, Browne. Archdeacons of Lincoln. *A Survey of the Cathedrals of York, Durham, Carlisle, Chester, Man, Litchfield, Hereford, Worcester, Gloucester, Bristol, Lincoln, Ely, Oxford, Peterborough, Canterbury, Rochester, London, Winchester, Chichester, Norwich, Salisbury, Wells, Exeter, St.David's, Landaff, Bangor and St. Asaph,* Vol. III (London: Osborne, 1742), p.100

Willis, F E d'A. Newstead Priory. *A History of the Parish of Uffington* (London, 1914), pp.25–34

Wright, Thomas (ed.). The Bishop of Lincoln to Cromwell. *Three Chapters of Letters Relating to the Suppression of Monasteries* (London: Camden Society, 1843), pp.94–95

Additional Bibliography

Bramley, J. *A short history of the religious houses of Nottinghamshire to the time of the Dissolution* (1948) <http://www.nottshistory.org.uk/bramley1948/contents.htm> [accessed 9 August 2017]

Burton, Janet. *Monastic and Religious Orders in Britain 1000–1300* (Cambridge: Cambridge University Press, 1994)

Clark, John Willis. *The Observances in use at the Augustinian Priory of S. Giles and S. Andrew at Barnwell, Cambridgeshire* (Cambridge: Macmillan and Bowes, 1897)

Coppack, Glyn. *Abbeys & Priories* (Stroud: Tempus, 2006)

Cownie, E. *Religious Patronage in Anglo-Norman England 1066–1135* (Woodbridge: Royal Historical Society, 1998)

Gasquet, Francis Aidan. *English Monastic Life.* Sixth edition (First published 1904) (London: Methuen, 1924)

Heale, Martin. *Norton Priory in Context: The Augustinian Canons in Medieval England* <http://docplayer.net/35744744-Norton-priory-in-context-the-augustinian-canons-in-medieval-england-martin-heale-university-of-liverpool.html>

Webb, EA. The Augustinian order. *The Records of St. Bartholomew's Priory and St. Bartholomew the Great, West Smithfield.* Vol. 1, pp.19–34 (Originally published by Oxford University Press, Oxford, 1921) In: *British History Online* <http://www.british-history.ac.uk/st-barts-records/vol1/pp 19-34> [accessed 7 January 2015]

Index

About the book

As with many other smaller houses of Augustinian canons in Britain, there are few visible remains of the medieval priory Newstead by Stamford at Uffington in Lincolnshire. Even its precise location is uncertain, the only clue being an array of enigmatic earthworks in open parkland at the west end of the parish. Originally founded as a hospital by William de Albini III in the late-twelfth or early-thirteenth century, it was dissolved in 1536. While information is scanty and widely dispersed, once pieced together, the picture emerges of a small but important priory which, in its heyday, was at the heart of the administration of the Augustinian order in Britain.

About the author

Nicholas J Sheehan was born in Sheffield. Following a career as a consultant rheumatologist in Peterborough and Stamford, he developed an interest in local history and he has published on several different subjects. Previous books include *Stamford University: the stuttering dream* and *Uffington in the County of Lincolnshire*. He lives in Uffington with his wife.

Cover image: Wax seal from Acknowledgements of Supremacy–Newstead by Stamford, 21 July 1534. Image supplied by The National Archives.

Cover by Mark Smith of Snipe Design